GHOST GUIDERS

THIRSTING FOR RESOLUTION

Lyneah Marks

Body Soul & Angels
Publishing

Lyneah@bodysoulandangels.com

ISBN : 978-0-9889827-5-8

If you have something that goes bump in the night and want a consultation for ECE™ or for personal growth, **the first 20 minutes are free for first time clients.** Contact me at

Lyneah@bodysoulandangels.com.
Facebook like: Body, Soul & Angels

Body Soul & Angels Publishing

DEDICATION

To my Mother who believed me.

To my family which motivates me, to my students who push me for more.

ACKNOWLEDGMENTS

I have a lifetime of experiences to thank for this book. The students in my Earth Healing Classes have motivated me to write and share these stories. I thank you all. I am grateful for all the experiences and validation that showed me ghosts are real and most of the time in need of assistance. I am grateful to Rudolph Steiner, Yogananda, the Stargate Community for teaching me equanimity of soul, how to live by love instead of fear and especially how to focus on positive directions so they will grow despite what it looks like in the world at this time. Deep gratitude to Natasha Haugen for her editing skills, to Jennifer Martin and Allysha for listening so wisely, and to Marc Harper for his support and editing skills.

FOREWORD

"I don't believe in ghosts," a white lab-coated PhD candidate, who had far more training in physics than I did, remarked one day while I taught in the Physical Science Department in West Virginia University's Graduate School.

"Why?" I inquired.

"Because I don't know anything that will go through a brick wall and rattle chains on the other side," he said pointing at the thick brick wall for emphasis. Mulling on this a bit, I responded,

"Well, correct me if I'm wrong, if I had an electromagnetic field generator and I projected a field through the wall and oscillated it, would it not rattle chains on the other side?" He turned quite pale and didn't speak to me for weeks.

Our sciences can measure things like ghosts and energy bodies, we just don't have the construct, as Piaget would call it. It is only 200 years since people were jailed and killed for outrageous ideas such as the sun is the center of the Galaxy. It's that recent in history that church and science separated. Science is not willing to get back in bed with religion, so it has steadfastly avoided anything that might indicate the existence of a soul because that might invite religion back in the door and heresy, hence punishment, might return. Breakthrough scientists have been attempting to dismantle these walls in the past few decades.

When I give talks about ghosts, it amazes me how many people come up to me after with their own stories. Society, science and logic says there are no such things as ghosts, but experience tells us otherwise. I think seeing ghosts is a little like color. Some people see all sorts of colors, others are color blind. Some people see ghosts and others are ghost blind.

We are generally frightened of ghosts. Why? Well, movies and stories have sensationalized the idea and the ones that are scary have made the greatest impression. What comes to mind when I say the word ghost? Something terrible that can hurt you? Aunt Bessie? *Casper the Friendly Ghost*? *Ghostbusters*? Most of the images are frightening. Funny as it was, *Ghostbusters* showed some scary spirits.

There are friendly ghosts who are often relatives who have died. They often have messages. Mine come most frequently at holidays or special events such as weddings, deaths, illness and births. This past Easter I felt a chill and a friend who was with me felt it too. She asked who that was and I turned inward to find a line of my relatives coming to say hello and to provide comfort. It was sweet.

Years ago, at my brother's wedding there was an apparently empty space to the right of center at the front. Several people suggested family fill in that space but most knew it was already occupied. My cousin and niece both commented that our deceased relatives were standing in that space. It was interesting that everyone, whether they were able to see ghosts or not, left that space open for the entire ceremony.

There are lost Disembodied Spirits (ghosts). They are people who have died but often they died suddenly and they are generally looking for something. Some are unaware they are dead, as explained in the movie *The Sixth Sense*.

I have been teaching Earth Healing Classes for many years – first in person, then over Zoom. By request, I started teaching classes on how to clear Disembodied Spirits and I often get requests to clear ghosts from houses and businesses. Realtors have hired me to clear properties that would not sell and after the clearing sold. I call it ECE™™: Energy Clearing and Elevation™. It's not just about clearing, it's also about raising the vibration level to one that benefits the third dimensional occupants.

"Do you watch the "Ghost Hunters" on TV?" asked one of my students.

"No, I don't watch most of them because they are sensational and looking to stimulate fear. They have no consideration for lost souls and no thought of how to help them. This is also largely true of the scientific groups who hunt ghosts to use their equipment trying to prove their existence. They too have little thought of how to help these lost souls. It brings me great joy to help them." While teaching /facilitating an Earth Healing Class, a particularly enthusiastic group asked me to create a class for going into greater depth on helping Disembodied Spirits, which inspired the creation of this book. I wondered if I had enough stories for a book. As you will see, I do, and there are many more stories not included here.

I have had a desire to place into general consciousness the

idea that Disembodied Spirits (AKA Ghosts) are generally lost souls, often tortured souls, who need assistance. This assistance is the subject of the Ghost Guiders Webinar. The stories herein are from my life and those of my students. Many more people are sensitive to the presence of ghosts than are ordinarily willing to admit. Many are touched by a loved one's presence sometimes in surprising ways after a transition. I have worked many years with hospice agencies and have heard many stories. Another reason for this book is to counter the influence of sensational ghost hunter programs, movies and groups. They seek to hunt not to help. My approach is one that assumes help is the purpose for paying attention to disembodied spirits. Another assumption is that if you are hearing or seeing disembodied spirits, you can probably learn to help them. If so, many ideas contained herein will help and if you wish more training and practice please contact me about the next Ghost Guiders Webinar: **Lyneahmarks@gmail.com** or text me at 919 949 3039. Even if you send an email, please text me to let me know you did as I receive so many emails. As we help disembodied spirits cross over, it helps Mother Earth because it lightens her load.

Even if you don't want to help, you may find the stories interesting. The first one takes place when I was 14 months old. I know I was that young because it was the Thanksgiving before my younger brother was born. I think many of us have early memories and if there is not an external source to date it, we assume we were at least 4 because that's what Psychology textbooks/classes tell us. I have met many people who have memories very early in life, even pre-natal memories. Strong emotional content imprints experiences into long-lasting memories. My mother's emotional response to me seeing a ghost, as you can imagine, was strong and made a huge impact on my young soul.

I do hope you enjoy these stories whether you are intrigued by ghosts or if you are looking to help souls become unstuck, to cross over and continue their journeys.

TABLE OF CONTENTS

Chapter 1

Childhood: The Sad Man

High–stemmed cobalt blue glass and silver-laced shrimp cocktail glasses stood on fancy white paper doilies. A fancy lace paper doily was their pedestal atop a pile of white china plates. Each place around Aunt Hay's perfectly appointed Thanksgiving table contained one, even my seat with the highchair at the corner, though mine was smaller. I stretched on tiptoe to admire the table with silver accents and pressed autumnal colored leaves. I could see my less than two-year-old face looking back at me. I reached for the large mirror-like spoon, and my Mother swiftly stopped my hand.

"Aunt Harriet works so hard to make this table perfect for Thanksgiving Dinner. Let's leave it that way until we are invited to the table," said my Mother, her voice gentler than her firm grip leading me to the living room once again.

We passed the mahogany sideboard covered with hot plates waiting to receive steaming dishes of turkey, turnip, mashed potatoes and sweet potatoes whose aromas made my tummy growl with hunger. I kept my hands at my sides even when I saw the pumpkin and mince pies promising sweet endings.

I wanted, like most children, to be engaged like my Mother, Aunt, and my teenage female cousins, but I was too little and was repeatedly told not to be underfoot in the kitchen. So, I ran from the dining room just outside the kitchen to the front door and back, reveling in the use of my legs.

"Dot, would you bring the Jell-o mold up from the basement?" Aunt Harriet called from the kitchen.

"Sure," Mom answered. "Come with me, sweetie." I took Mom's outstretched hand. We headed to the basement door.

My right hand held tightly to the wooden railing slightly over my head. My Mother's hand had a safe hold on my left with her slightly rough working hands. She walked in front of me carefully, watching her steps while patiently guiding mine. She looked so pretty. I loved her so much. We descended slowly into the basement, careful to protect our dress-up clothes. My younger brother wasn't there, and I thought my Mother was getting "fat" – but she was not fat; she was pregnant with him. He was born when I was 18 months old. This Thanksgiving was the one before he was born, which meant I was 14 months old. Once off the steps, Mom let go of my hand.

The single basement light cast interesting shadows as it swayed I looked around in wonder. Neatly stacked mysterious packages, closed storage bins, and covered furniture made for a treasure hunt if I were to be left alone, which I knew wasn't going to happen. My eyes rested on a sad man standing quietly in the corner. I wondered who he was and why he wasn't coming to dinner. He felt heavy with loneliness.

"Maybe he's been bad, and that's why he's in the corner." I thought. *"How sad. We should invite him to dinner; it would cheer him up."*

Stringy dark hair parted down the middle accented the length of his sad face which looked down at the floor. He only looked up at me for a moment. I felt his sadness like a cloud of energy touching my skin.

"Mommy, who's the sad man in the corner?" I asked innocently.

A gush of fear flashed through me like a little tornado as Mom looked in the direction I pointed. Mom swiftly swept me up in one arm, Jell–O mold held tightly in the other. She slammed the fridge shut with one foot and scurried up the stairs, putting me down at the top. She turned to firmly close the basement door before she popped me lightly on the butt saying,

"Go into the living room and stay there until you are called for dinner."

My Grandmother and Aunt Hay's grandmother sat there talking. I felt sad that I had scared Mommy, and I didn't understand why she wasn't inviting the sad man for dinner. I heard her whisper to my aunt in the kitchen.

"Lyneah just saw a ghost! She gasped in whispered tones. "Have you ever seen a man in the basement?" she asked my Aunt, sounding a bit out of breath.

"I haven't seen him, but Ellen has." Ellen was my 15-year-old cousin. "Ask Lyn to describe him later and we'll compare," she said in a low, conspiratorial tone. They stopped whispering abruptly when my tall Uncle leaned into the kitchen, asking how long it would be before dinner was served.

"Ghost?" I wondered. He looked like a man just like Uncle Mel or Dad, but more like a grandfather. Both my grandfathers were dead, but I had heard about them and wished I could have known my Mother's Father, who often regaled neighborhood children on the front porch with his stories. He was an adventurer who had sailed to China and back cow-punching across the United States before marrying Grandma. Mom said she thought his stories were mostly true. I knew I loved him. This man was neither of my grandfathers.

When Mom came out of the kitchen, she acted as if nothing had happened. Smoothing her apron, she called us to the table without looking directly at me.

"Bow your heads, please," began my Uncle solemnly. "Lord, we thank you for all the blessings you have bestowed upon us this year and this day. Bless..." His emotional grace was very long, and I was so hungry from all the enticing smells and sights. I squirmed in my highchair. I knew I should have closed my eyes, but I watched him. His eyes were damp when he concluded,

"Amen," and finally, we could all eat!

4

My Mother sat next to me and helped me eat a little of everything. We ate and ate. It was so good! I was done before everyone else, and my belly hurt. So, I got up and ran circles around the living room coffee table. After dessert, sitting alone on the back porch watching birds at the feeder, Mom came out and asked in a whisper,

"Honey, can you tell me what the man in the basement looked like?" she asked quietly. The women were clinking dishes and pans in the kitchen. The men were in the living room playing Pinochle. The Grandmothers were playing Bunco.

"He was soooo sad, Mommy… and he had funny hair."

"What made it funny?"

"It had a line like this," I drew on my head with my finger to indicate his thin hair parted down the center.

"What color was his hair?"

"Brown, it looked wet. He looked like a Grandfather."

"What did he wear, sweetheart?" asked my Mother, squirming in her seat. I could feel her discomfort though it did not come through her voice.

"A funny suit."

"What made it funny?"

"Big, with two buttons on each side" I pointed to my chest to

5

illustrate.

"That's called double-breasted honey. People used to wear those. How tall was he?"

"Like Daddy but fatter. He had funny shoes too."

"What kind of shoes?"

"Brown and a white sock on top."

"Oh, those are spats, old-fashioned shoes men used to wear. Anything else?"

"Mommy, why was he so sad? Was he bad?"

"OK, you go play with your cousins now," my Mom patted my butt again to direct me into the dining room, where Mom joined the women giving the silver a final polish. I sat coloring with my other cousin, Caryl, at one end of the table. I still didn't understand why Mom ignored this silent unhappy man. I was sure having dinner with us would have cheered him up, but I didn't ask again. I colored in silence.

"Maybe it's because he's a ghost, whatever that is," I thought.

I could hear my Mother and Aunt in the pantry.

"She said he had a double-breasted suit, thinning hair, spats, and he was about Roy's height but heavier," Mom whispered to Aunt Hay, thinking they could not be overheard. Roy was what they called my Dad.

"That's just how my daughter described that ghost!" whispered Aunt Hay.

"I wonder who he is," whispered Mom.

"Maybe I'll find out. Maybe he's someone who died in this house before we owned it. I'll contact the realtor this week."

"Ghost? Dead?" I suddenly realized he was not a flesh-and-blood person. Ghost meant dead. I knew Mom didn't want me to talk about it, so I didn't, but my questions churned on my very full stomach. I didn't want to frighten her any more than I already had, so I held my feelings and questions inside. His sadness touched my heart, and I genuinely wished to help him, but I was just a little kid. I earnestly wished I knew how.

"How many other people had I seen who were ghosts?" I wondered in confused silence, looking down at the lace on my pretty dress, comparing it to that of the doilies.

I wondered why my cousin and I could see him, but Mom and Aunt Hay couldn't. Why did they whisper? Why was this secret from the rest of the family? I was dizzy with questions but knew I had to stay quiet and obey my Mother. I colored and wondered.

*****

If it had not been such a special event and had my Mother not had such a strong emotional reaction, this might not have been so loudly imprinted in my early soul.

7

Outstanding events with major emotional impact are the strongest memories we have, and I have found that they are often earlier than we think. This incident could be set in time: the Thanksgiving before my brother was born. It had a date. Many memories do not. People share early memories with me when I share such stories. Perhaps you have a few.

This experience set an intention in my soul to help ghosts, and I believe that desire drew situations into my life that have taught me how to assist ghosts into a better place. It is very satisfying to guide souls to a place of rest and peace. My problem with ghost hunter shows, and scientific groups looking to document spirits, is they have no concept of helping them but often intend to stimulate fear. The opposite is needed in order to assist disembodied spirits. Fear needs to be overcome. Equanimity of Soul is required.

What does this have to do with Earth Healing, you might ask. Generally, lost souls (disembodied spirits or ghosts) carry some form of disturbance, trauma, or lower frequency energies. When you help them find a way to release those energies, progress and heal, you can clear the heavier energies they leave behind. As a result, you lighten Mother Earth's load. As a result, Gaia can more easily ascend to higher frequencies.

We learn and practice such techniques in the Earth Healing 101 webinar and the Ghost Guiders Webinar, to which this book is a companion. (see **www.bodysoulandangels.com** for more information).

Chapter 2

Haunted House

In a recent Earth Healing Webinar, a participant brought pictures of a house that she knew was haunted. It was in Vermont The home was a vacation home owned by her ex-boyfriend's family. Most of the time no one lived there full time. The participant and her ex were still friendly.

We brought daytime and nighttime pictures to show to the class. The night picture was first. It was naturally scarier. We did our openings, meditated and asked what was going on with this house. Many participants got different numbers of different things. I suggested we should first ask about the presence of any entities.

Entities are not fully formed beings. They are created out of strong emotions. There are anger entities, jealousy entities, rage entities, etc. Sometimes people can see the colors of entities. On the positive side you can have joy, bliss, ecstasy and love entities. There can also be entities of sexual energies. Entities tend to draw each other (like attracts like) and grow into larger and larger entities. They do not usually have an independent consciousness, rather they are driven by a primal urge to feed and grow. What they feed on is the same energy type that started them. When they run into like entities, they coalesce and grow stronger. At some point, they get large enough and able to stimulate the emotion that feeds them. For example, if you issue an angry energetic, an anger entity can attach to your little cloud of anger and if it is sufficiently evolved, it can give ideas that will make you create more anger. In this way the entity is fed. When we tuned in as a group and focused on the entities that were not for the highest good, participants reported many, possibly hundreds in and around the house. We started applying our energies to clear them and could feel an improvement after working on it as a group for about 5 minutes more.

When we reached consensus that this step had been completed, we turned our attention to disembodied spirits. How do we sense spirits? All the senses are possible. Some see spirits, some sense them tactically manifesting in chills or a sensation of cold. I know I have been pushed and guided by a sense of touch. Smell can be involved; I have heard stories of people smelling a person's favorite perfume or aftershave, a scent of coffee or tobacco in the room which is not physically present. The highest form of intuition is a "knowing". This is simply an awareness that something is there. The group opened their senses and tuned in. The report was that there were many disembodied spirits and we divided them into groups and created group clearings. There were many different stories including a group that died in a shipwreck. We listened to their stories and helped them cross over. Many seemed willing to do so after having their stories heard. The great part of working with a team is that some heard, some felt, some knew, some saw.

After clearing the last disembodied spirit, we did the elevation part of ECE™™ followed by putting a picture of the house under a crystal matrix to hold the energy.

In the next week, the "ex" went to the house. He was not a believer in energy or clearings but he was certain ghosts had always been in and around the house as long as his family owned it. Their family had multiple stories and many a family member had lost sleep trying to rest there. Everyone in his family had stories to tell about ghost experiences. The first night he stayed there after our clearing, he called to say he had the first goodnight sleep he's ever had in that house. He said the place felt quite different. He also reported that all the rodents were gone. We didn't even know it had a rodent problem. It appears that ECE™™ (Energy Clearing and Elevation™) left the house at a vibratory level that did not attract and support rodents. Isn't that interesting?

In addition, this house is on major ley lines and the clearing helped clear the ley lines as well. Many of the Disembodied Spirits were outside the house and some came from Revolutionary War times. When you clear one house, you sometimes clear the neighborhood, as we'll see later in this book.

Chapter 3

Scarlet Fever

My beautiful blue bedroom had a closet that I loved. It was underneath the stairs, and for me, it was a cozy place. It triangled back to a point behind two full racks of clothing. A beautiful old cedar chest full of extra blankets and pillows was in the back. When I opened it, the aroma of cedar filled the small space. My Mother was claustrophobic and I discovered that it was a perfect hiding place because it never occurred to her that anyone would want to be back there.

When I was about 8 or 9, I brought a book to the table just like my older brother had. "You can't bring a book to the table," my Mother informed me flatly.

She returned to bringing dishes from the kitchen to the dining room table. I knew it was no use to argue how unfair this was; I also knew injustice when I experienced it. So, when I was reading an exciting part when dinner was called, I used this hiding place to finish my Cherry Ames, Nancy Drew and Donna Parker mysteries stories. Mom and my Dad called and called at the front and back doors for me to come to dinner.

"Where is that child now?" my Mother asked.

"We're not waiting any longer," declared my Father followed by the noises of serving spoons scraping dishes.

I had more hunger for reading than for food. Using my flashlight, I stayed cozy on blankets and pillows, and finished my book. They assumed I had come from the front door when I appeared, probably because I opened and closed it tee hee. This way, a major injustice was righted in my mind.

My bed was opposite the closet, which had a folding door that was closed. A wooden dresser stood next to it. One night when I was four, my Mother and I were having our good night read and snuggle when I gasped surprise and asked,

"Mommy, who's the red man?"

I felt the waves of my Mother's freak out, and I regretted saying anything, but he so surprised me! He was all red: red wide-brimmed hat, red face, red shirt, red pants and a sweeping red cloak. He had a half-smirk half sneer that wasn't pleasant, but I didn't feel fear, just surprise. He ran from the closet, through my bed, and through me. My Mother didn't know what to say, so being of the generation that believed if you have nothing good to say, say nothing, she said nothing. I could feel her holding her breath.

"He's gone," I tried to comfort her. "Please finish the story," Mom resumed reading the story.

A few days later, I came down with Scarlet Fever. Many years later reading Elizabeth Haisch's book *Initiation*, I was surprised she mentions such beings. It is the only place I have seen reference to beings behind illnesses like this one. I know I saw other illness spirits as a child, but this was one of the memorable ones as it contained a strong emotional charge.

Have you ever seen such a being? What would you have done?

Chapter 4

Spirit On My Shoulder

When my 12-year older brother moved out to go to college, I inherited his bedroom in the front of the basement. I loved the solitude and being away from the noise of the living room television right outside my prior bedroom door. To access the basement, you had to go through the living room to the far side of the dining room to the stairs which descended into the basement. The spare refrigerator was on the left and two large wash tubs banked your right before you got to the long hallway.

I had very little interest in television. I didn't like the energy it emitted and most programs did not interest me. I preferred books that stimulated my imagination. It is interesting to note that Rudolph Steiner states that imagination is the organ of perception in the spirit world. What is happening to the youth who have everything shown to them in video games, TV, and movies? What will happen to them in the next life? Imagination is also critical to manifestation. A people without vision will perish, the Bible warns.

On the right, a previously ping pong room was now a junk room. On the left, the workroom leading to a storeroom was just before the old large oil furnace. A half bath with a pull chain toilet with a high wooden water box, a sewing area opposite a closet, and then the door to my bedroom with its own closet and two windows at ground level. Immediately outside my room was the sewing space which I loved having so handy.

Here's how I described this spirit encounter in Chapter 21 of *Thirsting for a Raindrop:*

THE NOISE THAT SAVES LIVES

The cozy cave-like privacy of my new room at the far end of the basement, after the upstairs Grand-Central-Station bedroom next to the only household TV and the front door entrance, was Nirvana for a budding pre-adolescent who revered quiet time. I thanked my older brother for moving out so I could inherit his room. I am sure he too was glad to be out from under the restrictions of the home turf. Carefully, I descended the basement stairs from the bright sunny dining room into the darkness leading to the steep basement steps. I always paused, remembering falling down these steps at a very young age. I passed the utility tubs where the wringer washer used to reside. My grandmother had caught her middle finger in a wringer leaving her nail a hard pointed mass difficult to file. The spare refrigerator dating back to the 50s or earlier still worked with its tiny freezer space. Then the turn to the main hallway with a junk room on the right where the ping pong table sometimes stood. The bathroom held a pull chain toilet complete with a raised wooden bowl. The smell of tobacco was heavy in the air as this was where My Father came to "think" and smoke.

Opposite, the furnace was halfway to my room. As I approached the furnace, I felt something on my right shoulder, and a noise started in my right ear like a truck passing on the highway: a high-pitched whine that didn't go down. The closer I got to the furnace, the louder the noise became. I walked back and forth several times, and each time the noise was loudest next to the furnace. "What does this mean?" I wondered. *"The furnace is going to blow up,"* was the clear answer that immediately entered my mind. Upstairs in the living room, I spoke to the newspaper sitting in the chair by the windows.

"Dad, please call the furnace man."

"Why?" the newspaper responded.

"The furnace is going to blow up." The paper never moved. Dad cleared his throat with a skeptical sound and said with disgust,

"Yeah, right kid! It's Summer, there's no need to call the furnace man." He shook the newspaper for emphasis without lowering it and returned his attention to perusing the news. I walked downstairs in silence. I thought about various courses of action and decided the only real control I had was to get out of the way of the explosion myself; this might let him know how serious I was. As I passed the furnace, the noise was louder than ever, and I felt the sense of urgency intensifying in my gut. I quickly packed my most precious possessions into two suitcases and struggled to get them through the door at the top of the basement stairs, past the dining room table and into the living room to the front hallway door. Only when I opened the door and started pushing the suitcases through did I hear,

"What do you think you are doing, young lady?" asked My Father, emerging from the Chicago Tribune's sports section showing the Cubs had lost yet again.

"I'm going to Jane's house two blocks away rather than Gaye's two doors away. When the furnace blows, it will take the whole block with it. You can stay here and die if you want to. I'm going," I said emphatically and returned to the job of moving my suitcases by myself.

Visibly annoyed, my Father folded his paper emphatically, walked to the dining room, and grudgingly called the furnace man. I stayed safely near the door with my packed bags close at hand. Half an hour later, a nice Polish man rang the doorbell. Dad took him downstairs, showed him the furnace, came back up and resumed reading his newspaper.

"*Bang!*"

Dad reached the downstairs door before I did and descended a few steps when the furnace man's white eyes shone through his blackened face.

"Mister, you're one lucky son of a bitch!" he reported. "That furnace had a stuck valve, and when I went to clean it, it blew! I don't know how you knew to call me. If you hadn't, that furnace would have blown sky-high by morning and taken the entire block with it," he left my stunned father on the stairs as he turned to complete the furnace cleanup.

I stood at the top of the steps feeling satisfied, entirely vindicated, maybe even a little smug, waiting for my Father to praise me for saving the life of eight families. When he turned, a drawn, angry face looked into mine.

"God damned witch!" was the only thanks I got as he pushed past me. I was too stunned to respond, too hurt to cry. I sensed he was frightened, but at that age, I was too young to understand why, or to know anything constructive to do with his response. I was sure he and the family would finally acknowledge my perceptions as real and valuable gifts now that there was empirical evidence. After all, weren't we a logical, scientific family? Crushed, my world took a spin. My heart hurt, and a chasm opened between my Father and me. It took many years and much inner work for that to heal."

* * * * *

I included this story because it was a disembodied spirit or a spirit guide who gave me that warning. I have wondered about these kinds of things in my life. Why did I and my ex jump up and dash across the room at an amazing speed just after receiving our good smelling food seconds before the heavy plaster and lathe ceiling fell in? One explanation is that our higher selves are not restricted by time and can see what's coming, so if we are in touch with our higher self and listening, it can warn us of disasters ahead. In the basement around the furnace, the impulse was not from inside me but outside. The noise was on my right shoulder, buzzing into my right ear. It had a presence. Later, during my near-death experience (Thirsting for a Raindrop Chapter Two, Otter Creek Wilderness) I learned that this presence, this energy signature, was my maternal grandfather, Fred Bobzin. It was his energy that warned me about the furnace.

It was his energy that told me everything would be fine when the brakes went out, and my Mother had to drive our Ford station wagon down a loop off-ramp into a very heavily trafficked major suburban Chicago intersection where the light had just turned red. All the traffic waited until we had passed across all six lanes without Mom having to blow the horn. She had reduced speed adequately to coast into a gas station on the other side, turned the engine off and pulled on the parking brake. The men who came out were stunned, asking if we knew how many accidents happen at that intersection per week. They both had watched what happened and agreed it was a miracle we made it through safely.

Grandpa Fred helped. So, there are those who can help from the beyond under certain circumstances. Grandpa Fred saved our lives at least three times I can pinpoint. For his guidance, I am deeply grateful.

The good news is I eventually healed the gap between My Father and me. It took a lot of work, and I am so grateful for my Soul Integration gifts which I learned partially from a deep desire to heal this relationship.

What to do about such spirit intervention? Listen. Be open and ask questions. I could have ignored the noise on my shoulder and if I had? Instead, I asked:

"What does this mean?"

We don't have to know we can just ask. Pay attention, ask, listen. That's the formula and for my family it saved lives.

Chapter 5

Mold Monster

When I saw *The Sixth Sense*, I was encouraged to see others saw such disembodied spirits. If you haven't seen this brilliant film, I highly recommend it. I continued to see them but turned my attention to more normal things most of the time. I knew they upset others in my family and I don't remember any until I took a year off from the University to help my brother, Ken.

The next major ghost appearance in my life happened in the appropriately named Erie, Pennsylvania. I gave myself cooking lessons by studying TV shows, including Julia Childs and the Galloping Gourmet. My grandmother did most of the cooking and would not have me in "her" kitchen, so I didn't learn anything about cooking. At age nineteen, I felt it was time to learn. Ken was a most appreciative audience, and I became quite an accomplished cook.

Certainly, I had enough experience to know that cheese should not mold in one day. We rarely ate leftovers in this house because they molded overnight. It didn't matter which store the food came from. I emptied the refrigerator, sterilized the inside with a bleach solution, and even used Q-tips to get under the seals. The next day new food was already molded. We double wrapped things like cheese and used airtight containers but things still molded quickly. Ken had also run out of helpful ideas.

One sunny afternoon I had gone up the stairs from the second-floor door into the unfinished attic and thought this would be a lovely artist's atelier. The next day I cleaned the space and set up my paints and canvasses with the expectation of hours in quiet solitude. I only painted one painting. It was very unlike my previous paintings. It was ugly, full of colors running into each other, creating dull dark sickening tones of greens, yellows, blacks, and reds clashing into a nauseating mess. After one canvas, I felt so uncomfortable I sprang up, gathered my paints, brushes, and materials, and in two swift trips, there was no trace of my artist's space left in the attic. My heart beating loud and fast, I firmly closed the attic door and put the ugly painting directly into the outside trash can. I did not even want to keep it to paint over.

After that, I noticed the creaks more. At first, they seemed to be normal older house sounds, but I slowly realized the creaks did not coincide with winds or storms but rather the time of day. Evenings, just after sunset, I would hear what seemed like something dragging across the floor. Sometimes I thought they were footsteps. I tried to calm my imagination and tell myself it was just something usual, but my gut sense wasn't buying that. The house was built of bricks and perhaps tree limbs were rubbing against them? I tried to push it aside as not my problem and focused on what Julia Child was preparing that day.

Downstairs, the living room couch was opposite the staircase. The television sat on a coffee table pushed against the wall beneath the stairs. Wooden spindles were spaced so you could see the wall behind the stairs. To get to the kitchen, you had to come down the stairs, pull a U-turn, and walk through the living room. Watching a show one evening, relaxing after cleaning up from dinner, I smelled and felt it first. It smelled, well, moldy. It looked like something out of the movie *Ghostbusters*, which was yet to be produced two decades later. I named it the mold monster. It was a gooey, drippy mess of a being. Awful greens, yellows, greys, and blacks, much like the painting in the attic, were mounded into a thing about six feet tall that undulated more than walked. It was more than two feet wide. With amazement more than horror, I watched as it came down the stairs with no appendages apparent. Pulling my knees toward me, I lifted my feet off the floor to ensure I didn't contact any part of its energy. It came down the stairs, turned the U, slimed across the living room, past the TV, and into the kitchen, not even noticing me on the sofa. I could see it with my eyes open. A wave of nausea flowed through me as it passed. It looked like someone had repeatedly regurgitated and stuck it all together into a tall mound. I immediately knew it was what was making the food in the refrigerator mold.

I didn't know what to do, and I wasn't going to tell anyone about it either. I said some prayers. A week later, my friend, John, was sitting next to me watching television. I saw the mold monster and turned to see his face with a surprised, hesitant stare.

"Tell me what you see," I demanded.

"Nothing," he said, shaking his head in denial, never taking his eyes off the Mold Monster, which I was sure he was seeing.

"You have to tell me because I need to know if we are seeing the same thing."

He looked at me and could see I needed his confirmation.

"It looks like a pile of nasty moldy compost."

"Exactly!"

"What can we do about it?" I asked earnestly.

"I don't know, but I have someone I can ask," John said as he left quickly. The monster made its way to the kitchen again.

John called later to convey what his friend recommended. The best he had to offer in 1970 was to wait until I knew the creature was in the attic and take a blue sheet, tack it up quickly, covering the attic entry about three steps up from the door, leaving enough space to place a Bible with a gold cross on top of it. I did this, and afterward, things no longer molded in the refrigerator. When we moved out of that house, I removed the Bible, cross, and sheet, feeling guilty at leaving the mold monster for the next occupants. Many years later, when I learned how, I cleared that house.

At age nineteen, I didn't even know what category to put this thing into. It didn't seem to have a consciousness like disembodied spirits or nature spirits (elves, dwarves, gnomes, sprites, and fairies). I now think that it was probably a collection of entities originally created by strong emotions and that it did not have a human type of consciousness. Nevertheless, it did seem to clear in the way entities can be cleared. Perhaps it was initially created by someone sick – someone with strong feelings about throwing up.

Have you ever suddenly felt something you know is not yours? You may have run into an entity. They exist for positive emotions as well. For those who are unaware of what thoughts are theirs, and what thoughts come from other places, they can feel the entity energy is their own. If it creates, for example, anger, then it feeds and grows. People who are stuck in anger can have entities attached to them. I have generally found that early forming entities are easy to clear. Larger, more developed entities can be complex and require more advanced techniques.

Generally, a simple technique can be used to clear entities. I first read about it in a good read called: *Behaving as if the God in All Life Mattered* by Michaelle Small Wright. She recommends working with angels at each corner of spiritual white sheets (tablecloths or fabric). Ask the guides of your choice to run the sheets from below through the building (at least one spirit at each corner, more for larger buildings). Ask for all things that do not serve the highest good that can be removed to be removed. St. Germain is a good one to ask to transmute what is removed back to source energy or love. You need to stay with them, imagining the cloth coming through the building. It usually takes multiple cloths. For large institutions that haven't been recently cleared, if ever, it can take dozens. Generally, entities can be removed and transformed in this way since they are not true sentient beings. This technique is wonderful to use in public places of high stress: schools, hospitals, nursing homes, rehab facilities, jails, and courthouses, to name a few. Many churches can benefit from this technique as well.

If you have something that goes bump in the night and want a consultation for ECE™ or for personal growth, **the first 20 minutes are free for first time clients.** Contact me at

Lyneah@bodysoulandangels.com.
Facebook like: Body, Soul & Angels

Rudolf Steiner's Meditation Techniques Teaches Us Mindful Meditation

Brief Description: Great meditation exercises for beginners and for advanced alike. Considered safe even for a novice, these exercises build spiritual organs of perception...Dr. Steiner in *Knowledge of Higher Worlds'* said that these exercise comprise a safe spiritual path if you observe two things: first, your motives must be other than self-centered. You must be doing this for higher reasons that just your personal gain. Second, you must have great patience with yourself...This may sound easy, but you will likely experience challenges in providing yourself with the time to grow along this journey...

More information on these exercises are sprinkled throughout this book and the entire post can be found at http://www.bodysoulandangels.com/five-basic-exercises

You are welcome to download the entire section for free.

Chapter 6

Persistent Shocking Image

Tall and stately, Uncle Mel was my Father's older brother and my only living Uncle. Successful in business, he became the VP and comptroller of a prominent Chicago Michigan Avenue bank. He was a serious man most often, with a contentious relationship with my Father, his brother, who seemed jealous of my Uncle's success and felt the world had dealt him a lousy hand. He seldom talked about it; he just exuded an energy of resentment toward life in general and my Uncle in particular, often resulting in tension at family gatherings. His first wife, Aunt Harriet, had a great sense of humor and would often break the ice with her quips and jokes. With my Mother's help, the women kept the peace. Into my late teen years, we spent all the major holidays together.

Aunt Harriet died suddenly of an anaphylactic response when I was 19. My Uncle was devastated. It had never occurred to him that she would go first. He was a man who felt deeply but generally held it in, and now he was like a baby gushing tears or sitting in a state of emptiness. I moved into his house for a few weeks to help my cousin Caryl care for him. Uncle Mel didn't know basic things about the daily functioning of the house. The washer and dryer were a complete mystery to him; he didn't even know how to work the stove or oven. I watched him over breakfast one morning as Caryl prepared food. Sitting at the table, he was tense, silently crying, his large hands wrapped around a glass of orange juice. Then, staring blankly into space, he started to shake, and the glass crushed between his hands, cutting them. Blood and orange juice spurted across the table as his repressed anger exploded unexpectedly out of his despondency.

It was some time before he made it through the stages of grief and found a woman he liked enough to marry. She was nice enough. They moved into her house, keeping his house in Oak Park, Illinois. When he passed, she survived him. I drove from West Virginia to Chicago to attend the funeral. Once there, whenever I closed my eyes, I saw a vision of my Uncle in a small cement block room with tiny windows at the top of the walls, like a prison. He sat on a three-legged wooden stool that was way too small for him. His head and part of his face were covered in black leather. It covered his forehead and eyebrows tightly and came to points on his cheeks with slits for his eyes revealing haunting, hollow, sad eyes. It looked like something out of an S & M catalog. I could feel he was punishing himself for some reason. He had put himself in this etheric prison between dimensions.

I was twenty-nine and tried to ignore it, but I couldn't sleep. Every time I closed my eyes, Uncle Mel's tragic ones stared at me. It wasn't a still image, but a video. He sometimes moved or looked up or down slightly. I could feel he desperately wanted something, but I didn't know what. My fear caused me to open my eyes, and I was exhausted from lack of sleep. My cousin Caryl suggested I come to his Oak Park house with her to keep her company while she went through his things. Maybe I would get more information, I thought. I now wanted to know what he wanted. I curbed my fear and went to the familiar house where Thanksgiving dinners had been held throughout my childhood. When I tried to sleep in his old bed, I saw him with my eyes open in the mirror! That's when I jumped up and told Caryl about the visions.

"We are trying to find the pre-nuptial agreement," Caryl confided. "Please ask him where it is."

I agreed, and the answer I got from him was,

"Look in the safety deposit box." I conveyed this to Caryl.

"We've already looked. It's not there. His wife is giving us little things like an antique Polaroid camera acting as if all his assets belong to her. I've seen the prenup. Everything that is his goes to his heirs, and everything that is hers goes to hers. We just can't find it, and until we do, we are SOL. My sister is relying on that inheritance for the kids' education. You know the extenuating circumstances around that."

I asked him again and again and got the same answer. I reported I had nothing new, just the same vision and something about a safety deposit box. Could there be another one? Caryl finally remembered a box her Dad had opened for her years ago when she started college. She didn't even know if it still existed. She searched and found the key, went to the box, and there was the pre-nuptial agreement! I was so relieved to sleep that night without images of Uncle Mel in that prison cell he had constructed out of his guilt and concern for things to be set right.

I had to find Equanimity of Soul to hear what Uncle Mel wished to say. It was a shaky state for me at that age, but I got close enough to hear his basic message. I had to overcome fear repeatedly with the disturbing image he projected. An Uncle I knew to be in control and on top of things most of his life appearing in that fashion was shocking, and I responded with fear. I wanted the vision to go away, but when it did not, I had a stronger need for sleep and a desire to help my family. Had I been able to be calmer, maybe I would have heard more details sooner. Years later, in an exercise at a Jean Houston workshop, I received thanks from my Uncle Mel and a precious feeling of respect I had not experienced from him in physical life.

Ghosts with messages can be persistent. Equanimity of Soul is critical to being able to communicate with them. In later years as I have continued to mature spiritually, I have been better able to find equanimity in the face of harrowing visions, feelings, and experiences. The Five Basic Exercises of Rudolph Steiner have helped greatly. As part of the Earth Healing and Ghost Guiders webinars, I ask everyone to do these exercises, for they build the spiritual organs of perception, including Equanimity of Soul. You can find them and a schedule of classes at **www.bodysoulandangels.com**.

If you have something that goes bump in the night and want a consultation for ECE™ or for personal growth, **the first 20 minutes are free for first time clients.** Contact me at

Lyneah@bodysoulandangels.com.
Facebook like: Body, Soul & Angels

Chapter 7

A Ghostly Painting

The next ghost in my life that stands out in my memory came in the form of a painting. Here are excerpts from Thirsting for a Raindrop, Chapter 41, Susan On A Balcony:

* * * * *

I was so excited to land my first professional job at Montgomery Ward's Training Department…I was delighted to find a career path based on my education. I had a fancy title: Computer Assisted Instruction Developer! I soon learned that despite a title, a five-foot-high cubicle in a vast old windowless building felt more like a prison cell than an office. Mostly, I liked my work. I enjoyed developing the training modules and learning about new things.

Before long, the main event of the day was our lunchtime visits to the Bargain Basement. We walked through a vast tunnel under Chicago Avenue, allowing us to avoid weather and traffic. The entrance to the Bargain Basement felt like a bomb shelter entrance, but what a place for a treasure hunt! One day Eileen, Pam and I went over, laughing on our way. We split up, each attracted to a different area. I turned down the first aisle and BOOM! My heart started racing and pounding loudly. Goosebumps covered my body; the tension in my chest was binding. I could barely breathe. What frightened me so? It was a painting! No lions, tigers, or wolves, just an impressionist painting of a pleasant-looking young woman with strawberry blonde hair, dressed in white, seated in a Bombay-style wicker chair on a Paris balcony with one gloved hand on a little Yorkshire terrier in her lap. Her turned face was almost smiling, and a fancy white ruffled hat sat atop her head. My logical mind said nothing was frightening about this painting, but the rest of me said, "RUN!!!!!!!" and I did.

I sprinted out of the store through the tunnel, and only slowed when I entered the hallway leading to our office cubicles. I was twenty-two and trying to be Ms. Logical Computer–Assisted–Instruction Developer. It was my first professional job, and I wanted to fit in.

My co-workers returned and asked what was wrong.
   "Nothing," I quickly snapped way too firmly. "I just had to go to the bathroom, but I'm fine now," I said in a softer voice. I did not want to talk about it, so I pretended to have a lot of work to do.

The next day, I went to the Bargain Basement as usual with Eileen and Pam, but I cautiously avoided the aisle the painting had been on and turned down a new one, only to find the painting at the end of this one! Its powerful spell raced my heart again, and I found it difficult to breathe. I fled, later claiming ongoing bowel problems, which I was starting to have. This occurrence went on for five days in a row, with a different aisle each day. Each day I avoided all the aisles down which I had previously seen the painting and – boom! There was this nice impressionist painting causing me a panic attack again and again. It made no logical sense, but even my logical, scientific, just–studied–statistics mind knew it was way beyond chance probability.

That Friday, Eileen cornered me and told me I had to tell her what was going on.

"I'm not buying the diarrhea story anymore," she said, standing in front of me with one hand on each arm of my chair. After several refusals and attempts at diversion, her unyielding gaze got me to explain finally the reaction I was having to the painting. She calmly said, "I'll see if there is more than one painting."

"Brilliant! Why didn't I think of that? There must be dozens of those reproductions," I said with relief.

Eileen returned, reporting there was only one. I was disheartened. "By the way, it's a Cassatt, and it's called Susan on a Balcony Holding a Dog," she reported. "Sorry. I know you'd hoped for dozens." I nodded and said nothing, trying to push down the torrent that tried to rise from my gut.

My waking and sleeping dreams were filled with images of the woman in this painting, and I vowed not to go to the bargain basement again until Susan's image was gone. After a weekend of not being able to stop thinking about this painting awake or asleep, I was eating lunch alone at my desk when Eileen returned from the bargain basement a little out of breath.

"It's gone," is all she had to say.

I sprang up from my desk, sprinted over to the Bargain Basement, and scoured the place. My intensity caused the manager to emerge from her one-way glass office to ask if she could help me. When I described the painting, she said, "Oh, I'm sorry, that sold this morning. Would you like me to see if I can find you another one?"

"No!" I said, a little too forcefully, then corrected my tone. "Oh, no, thank you, that's quite all right. Thank you so much, but that will not be necessary."

I felt relief wash over me, and I left feeling a wash of gratitude that it was finally gone. On the way back to my desk, one of the department artists called my name as I passed.

"Stop by for a minute. I have a picture of you," she said innocently. She was famous for caricaturing people, and I had looked forward to seeing one of me. I put my things in my office and returned to the artist's space. She pulled out the Cassatt painting and said, "Doesn't she look just like you?" Way too loudly, I screamed, "Get that thing away from me!!!!!!!!!!!" and ran back to my cubicle.

One did not scream in the Montgomery Ward Corporate Headquarters. People came from many departments away to find out what the commotion was. The artist showed each of them the painting, asking if they didn't see me in it. The overwhelming agreement was that she could be my twin sister. Internally I screamed as each person came to my cube to tell me how much I looked like Susan. I was disturbed and bothered that I was upset. I turned my desk to face the corner, my back to the cubby opening and stuffed two broken cigarette filters in my ears for plugs. I pretended to be deeply involved in writing. Before leaving that night, I stopped in the artist's office, kept my composure and asked politely,

"Would you please take that painting home with you? I can't explain it, but I'd like never to see it again," she shrugged and put it behind her drawing table. She stared at me but said nothing. In my naiveté, I interpreted the head nod to mean she would take it home.

That night, through broken sleep, I realized in the morning, I had been dreaming of the painting all night long. The dreams were so vivid, so real, so alive. Each time I woke, I felt I was living Susan's life instead of my own. In the morning, I felt like I needed another night to sleep.

The next day, my Mother came to have lunch with me at my place of employment for the first and only time in my entire life. After lunch, I introduced her to various people in the department. In the art room, the artist closest to the door nodded at Mom from behind her drawing table, reached over, pulled the painting from behind the table where she had placed it yesterday, and said, "Doesn't this look just like your daughter?"

"Oh, yes," my Mother agreed. "It's yours for five dollars."

"I must have it!" Mom pulled $5 from her purse, traded it for the painting, turned, and GAVE IT TO ME!!!

Internally I was screaming. This painting was out to get me, and apparently, it had won. Why had it come to me, and what did it want? The only weird story I knew about a painting was The Portrait of Dorian Grey, in which Dorian's evil deeds appear in his portrait. Yet, he remains young and handsome as his portrait becomes increasingly uglier. Defeated, I took the painting home and placed it in the most remote closet of my apartment. Occasionally I checked to see if it had started to age or have ugly marks. It didn't, and I didn't know whether to be relieved or disappointed. If that was not it, then what was the purpose of this painting in my life?

The painting faded into the background until eight years later. Long gone from Chicago, settled in West Virginia, Don and I had been actively trying to become pregnant for three and a half years. Having explored all the medical options, I turned to meditation. I meditated regularly, focusing on the question, "What do I need to do to get pregnant and birth a child?"

On several occasions when I meditated longer, a remarkably deep grief emerged from the abdominal pain areas the doctor had told me were imaginary.

Tuning into this anguish was neither easy nor comfortable. Driven by curiosity and an overwhelming desire for a child, I rode the waves of grief and pain as long as I could stand it. Crying and sobbing shook my entire being. Lying down seemed to accentuate my ability to access the suffering. I wondered at the depth of the mourning because nothing to date in my life warranted such a deep level of grief. Susan appeared in my meditations, standing sad and silent as if she held some deep dark secret. I usually stopped exhausted and sweat-soaked. It took an effort to come out of it. I decided to research the painting. Maybe that would help unlock its mystery.

*****

Early Summer misty morning Washington DC air flooded over me as I paced before the impressive golden Beaux-Arts Corcoran entrance doors. I wondered what, if anything, I would learn from Mary Cassatt's original painting. It was a weekday, and I paced alone, excitedly waiting for the doors to open. When the guard opened the huge doors, I entered, aware of lively butterflies in my belly. No one had to tell me where the painting was. I could feel it, and my heart pounded harder as it drew me closer.

I paused in a hallway, knowing I was on the back side of the painting. Heart racing, I drew a deep breath, attempting to center myself, before entering the salon. Bam! The effect of the painting hit me like a wave of strong Chicago wind as I faced the original. I jumped back at the strength of my visceral response and fell onto the sleek wooden bench. My heart raced, my brain felt it might explode, my stomach did flip flops, and goosebumps covered my entire body head to toe. There sat Susan, posing on the balcony with the dog. As I stared at this image, it seemed to come to life and morph into a movie. I watched Mary Cassatt while she painted, and people came in and out of her apartment to silently view her work. I followed them inside and watched a woman with her hair pulled back in a neat bun. She spoke with a dark-haired, bearded man and a matronly well-dressed, dark-haired woman. I took notes of the details I saw in my visions: the rug patterns, the curios' placements, the orientations of the rooms, and as I tuned into the conversations, I noticed they were speaking German. *"Ah hah!"* I thought, *"That must be wrong. I don't know much about Cassatt, but I do know she was an American living in Paris. Why would an American in Paris speak German?"* I was sure I'd find this incorrect, and that one error would allow me to discount all this bizarreness.

Follow–up research verified details of the visions I had while sitting in front of the original painting. I flipped through every book I could find about Cassatt. I spent time in libraries and the National Archives. Descriptions, photos, and renderings showed the woman with the bun to be Mathilda Valet, Cassatt's concierge, trusted adviser, and the aunt of the painting's model: Susan. The bearded man was Cassatt's father and the woman was Cassatt's mother. What surprised me was that French law of that era strongly favored French domestics who could 'steal their employers blind' and get away with it. One source reported French domestics at that time could not be fired for anything short of homicide. This law was an overreaction to an era when they had no rights. It did not apply to domestics from other countries. Because of this, Mary Cassatt hired only Alsatian and German help, so they spoke German in her apartment! I could not think of a way I could have known this. I had been drawn to Impressionist art since my first childhood visit to the Art Institute of Chicago, where I fell in love with Monet's Haystacks and came to know them as friends. I never studied impressionism and I knew nothing about Cassatt prior to this research. Thanksgiving weekend 1981, I made my way to Roslyn, Vermont for Jean Houston's Possible Human Retreat. The weekend turned out to be one of the most expansive, fun, creative experiences of my life. Jean led us through an Ericksonian-style meditation to the top of a mountain, through a door to explore a bigger–than–life sweet green pepper. Then down, down, down, stairs. Through hallways leading to a field, to a river, and into a beautiful, safe boat that floated down the river until it gently deposited me on a beach. All this was designed to bring us to deeper levels of our subconscious minds. As the vision continued, Jean stopped guiding us verbally and allowed our subconscious to guide us.

I walked the narrow end of a two-by-four across a bog to dry land where I waited for my guide, who was a skeleton (symbol of intellect) riding a horse. I knew he was Lancelot, and he offered me a beautiful gold jewel-studded chalice. I noticed the gold rope surrounding each jewel encircling the chalice: amethyst, ruby, emerald, and sapphire. I drank deeply of the dark purple substance it contained. When I finished, Lancelot swooped me onto his steed. I held tightly around his waist as we swept into the air, across time and space. He navigated the horse smoothly forward until we sped toward the ground, stopping perfectly just outside a white picket fenced yard somewhere in the

Black Forest of Germany, maybe a hundred years ago based on the clothing I now wore in the vision. There was a lovely four-year-old blonde girl in the yard and Lancelot said,
"Stay and play with her awhile."

I looked into her beautiful blue eyes, thinking she looked vaguely familiar. We played without words for a time, and then she spoke to me in German, saying simply, "Come," and she took my hand.

We magically flew across time and space, landing on a balcony in Paris where she was now age 17, posing for Mary Cassatt with the little Yorkshire terrier in her lap. I now knew it was 1883, and she was Susan. She took my hand again, and we flew across the ocean to somewhere outside Philadelphia, to a wedding lace trim house where Susan had just died in childbirth. Her spirit stood outside her dead body, and her dark-haired husband, the railroad baron in the Degas portrait I had seen at the Pittsburgh Museum, was cleaning the crying baby through his own tears. Susan's spirit, now separate from mine, was wracked with grief and pain. It was a relief not to feel the grief from inside for a change. Lancelot asked me to comfort her and tell her it would be all right. I turned to do so, became quite attached to her emotions, and the lines between us blurred. I turned back to the grand knight and said, "She has every right to be hysterical – she just died in childbirth!" Our souls started to meld again, and I felt her pain, suffering, and grief as mine. Lancelot separated us. Standing boldly between us, he held our hands and said,

"Come, look and listen," as he led us slowly across time and space. As he did, we watched the baby grow into a lovely young woman.

We both sighed deeply and felt, "Oh, it is all right." Susan and I felt a huge release. With that, her spirit, separate from mine, lifted and soared with her angels into the Light. I felt her send waves of gratitude our way. I thanked Lancelot and the vision faded.

Coming back to a more standard consciousness, I felt tremendous relief and accomplishment…That was Thanksgiving weekend. The detox process from the after-effects lasted through the end of January, and after the very next opportunity, I got pregnant.

* * * * *

This rather dramatic experience opened my thirty-one-year-old eyes to many things: reincarnation, soul relationships, the power of visions, and more. I overcame my fear which allowed me to open to things that would enable me to understand the purpose of this "ghost" of a painting and draw the experiences and ideas into my life which helped me heal. It gave me access to the Akashic Records, where the information of all that has happened resides. It helped me free Susan's soul, possibly an aspect of my own soul. It helped me move forward on my path. It resulted in a daughter whom I love deeply.

How many times have you just ignored something that didn't fit your current perception of reality? How many "ghosts" have you ignored in your lifetime?

Rudolf Steiner's Meditation Techniques Teaches Us Mindful Meditation

Exercise 1: Concentration - Make a mental picture of some simple object, for instance, an ordinary pencil with an eraser on one end. Excluding every other thought, and feeling, ask yourself questions such as, "What is it made of?" "How is it put together?", etc. so as to keep the mind pinned to the one point of interest. Or take a simple phrase like, "Rain freshens the air." and maintain it for 5 minutes. Keep watch for ideas trying to break in on your train of thought... continued at http://www.bodysoulandangels.com/five-basic-exercises

Chapter 8

Sad Boy

I mostly cooled my jets about ghosts and spirituality in general the first years of college — well actually through my first corporate jobs. I had the misguided late adolescent early adulthood desire to fit in and be normal. I lived in buildings that did not have ghosts during that time. I was working hard to be a professional. As you may have read in Thirsting for a Raindrop, unusual things kept happening to me including when I moved to Bethesda, MD outside Washington DC, where ghosts reappeared. A sad young boy stood in the same place on the stair landing to the upstairs. I sent him love but still didn't know what to do to help him. I never mentioned it to anyone but several of my friends took me aside and asked who the boy was on the staircase. More disturbing, they described him just as I saw him. I just learned to live with him. I could feel his sadness, but we never communicated. During this time, I had a Halloween. We spent days setting up and creating spooky recordings, decorating and setting up sound systems. I dressed as a fortune teller and had a booth on the dimly lit porch contained by blankets, sheets, cloths and aluminum foil streamers. You had to enter through an aluminum foil tunnel on the stairs. It was not an easy entrance. Microphones In the tunnel connected to a reverb PA system gave you back repeating whatever you said.

"What the hell," came back as "What the hell, what the hell, what the hell." It was majorly amusing.

I started reading people's palms as a joke. I had never done this before. When I was about 15, my Mother encouraged me to let an Indian man read my palm at the doctor's office where my Mother worked and I sometimes helped. He was quite accurate about past and present things and my Mother wrote down the future predictions which unbeknownst to me she kept in a Bible. Years later she brought it out showing me how accurate he was!

Many came for me to read their palms. I started looking at the hand of someone I didn't know and said whatever popped into my mind. She was pretty impressed and started saying,

"How did you know that?"

I stopped "reading" because people said I was accurate. My new approach to a reading was to look deeply into someone's palm and say,

"Oh, there's a crack, (long pause) and there's a crack (more pause) and there's a crack," play slapping at the person's face clapping my hands on the last one and sent them on their way. I abandoned my booth for the rest of the party.

I worried about the young man, but I didn't want to deal with him and I regretted that even at the time. Years later when I learned how to help Ghosts cross over I did a meditation, found him in the ethers,

"Hello, can you hear me?"

"Yes."

"I've come to talk with you. Do you remember me?"

"Yes, you used to live in this house."

"I'm sorry it's taken me so long."

"It's OK, most people don't even see me," he said sadly. "You did. That helped. I could feel you saw me and that made me feel real."

"I'm so sorry I didn't help you before, I was afraid and I didn't know how. What's your name?"

42

"Bobby."

"What do you need, Bobby?" I asked in a kind voice.

"I want my Mother," he said urgently. He appeared to be 8 or 9 years old. He was well dressed for his age but there was something traumatic as well – his head appeared injured. I wanted to ask what happened, but I felt his need was so intense, I asked angels to find his mother and a golden light portal opened behind him. A woman stood in the golden light portal between two angels.

"Turn around and see if that's her," I suggested and he turned. His countenance lit up and he sprinted with long strides toward her. She opened her arms to receive him. I watched as they embraced and the portal closed. I felt relieved at their reunion. I didn't know what injured his head but it didn't matter. He was in the light and with his mother. My heart felt warm and grateful that I could finally help him.

Rudolf Steiner's Meditation Techniques Teaches Us Mindful Meditation

Exercise 2: Controlling the Will - Choose some simple act you would not ordinarily do at the time of day you determine, such as carrying a sofa cushion to a chair in the next room, turning your ring around on your hand, rubbing your nose or pulling your ear. It needs to be something without meaning or value, merely arbitrary. To do this requires releasing an impulse deep inside of you that prods you to remember what you have chosen to do at the given time, then DO IT, daily at the same time. This way you are learning to obey your own commands, training your will forces. The more trivial the action the more difficult it is to arouse the will to do it -- without fail,…continued at http://www.bodysoulandangels.com/five-basic-exercises

Chapter 9

Butt End of the Rifle

While in Arizona, we were guided to look for a home in Cordes Junction, a small community North of Phoenix. I 17, the main highway North out of Phoenix crosses State Route 69 West to Prescott. We were drawn there originally when our friend Joseph visited and we stopped on the way back from Sedona. We righted two giant vortices (both had to be reversed). We accomplished this as a group (Joseph, Marc, Carolyn and I). After that Marc and I were still drawn to that area and viewed several places as potential homes.

The realtor called saying she had the perfect property for us. I met her midweek on a pleasant, sunny day. It was a beautiful piece of property with a few acres backing up on hundreds of acres of BLM (Bureau of Land Management) property, meaning no one could build there. Despite the sunshine the property looked dark. The house was lovely but it also looked dark. Inside it was especially dank and stuffy. Out back a long dog run, an outdoor jacuzzi, out buildings and room for tennis courts completed an impressive property if you just looked at the physical aspects. It really should have been the perfect property but it didn't feel right from the very beginning. The realtor apologized saying the family was inside the house. They were too sick to go anywhere. I later learned they had fallen ill after moving into this house, lost their jobs as a result and had to sell. I wondered about that. It made for a very unusual showing.

Inside, the family sat mesmerized by the tv. They all looked drugged or ill and depressed close to catatonic. They were all seriously overweight and their coloring was greyish. The parents and two children were all sitting in the living room and they barely registered that we were there. The realtor brought me through, showed me the house and I went through as quickly as possible. I was anxious to get outside again. I told the realtor that I would get back to her after talking with my husband. I said a quick goodbye, went to the car and watched her drive off. When she was out of sight, I returned to the house and from the car I asked,

"OK. Who is here?" and waited.

A salty old miner leaning on his rifle pointing into the dirt came into view and said,

"I killed her, I killed her with the butt end of my rifle. She'll never forgive me."

He was just short of 6 feet tall, with disheveled hair, dirty, dusty coveralls and a plaid shirt. This was topped by a dusty, black crushed wide-brimmed hat. He was unshaven as if frozen in time. He spoke with a thick country-style accent which I heard clearly inside my head.

I did my opening, turned inward and asked my guides how I could help this man. In my inner sight I saw a portal of brilliant golden light appear. A woman stood with her hands on her hips. She wore an ankle-length country style old fashioned dress. I got the knowing that she was his wife. So, I said to him,

"Why don't you turn around and ask her?" He looked confused then turned to look.

"Betsy is that you?" he said incredulously.

"Yeah, your old coot get over here," she hollered in a similar accent which indicated they were from somewhere in the South and gestured for him to come that way.

"Well!!! I never thought you'd forgive me."

"You just don't know anything! Come over here and I'll tell you all about it. We had a contract for that to happen and I'll explain everything, just come on."

He started to go toward her and the light. When he came close, she hit him on the shoulder.

"You can't bring that rifle with you - leave it back there," she commanded gesturing toward the ground.

He obediently placed the rifle on the ground, still looking quite surprised at her presence. He came toward her again and she hit him on the shoulder again and said,

"You say thank you to the nice lady."

He turned around, tipped his hat in my direction still looking dazed and said,

"Thank you ma'am."

He followed her into the light, she nodded thanks to me, put a hand on his shoulder and turned her attention completely onto him. Her face showed gratitude, relief and joy at having him back. The portal closed as they walked off talking. I stayed for about an hour clearing the grey, sticky energy he had created around this house. I was reasonably certain it was the cause for the family's illness. St. Germain and angels helped clear the almost knee-deep yucky slime. In some parts of the movie, ghost busters had it right!

1848 had been the start of the California Gold Rush and a large migration of people moving West. That miner had been there for over a hundred years. How lovely to be able to help him find rest and resolution with his wife, likely a soul mate of many lifetimes. Also, a joy to be able to help the family.

47

Although I never followed up on this and I don't know exactly what happened, I am reasonably certain they got better and that it was much easier to sell the house after this clearing. I have seen the results of such clearings on families health and well being and it is visible in some cases and reported in others.

If you have something that goes bump in the night and want a consultation for ECE™ or for personal growth, **the first 20 minutes are free for first time clients.** Contact me at

Lyneah@bodysoulandangels.com.
Facebook like: Body, Soul & Angels

Body
Soul &
Angels
Publishing

Chapter 10

Metal Spiders from the Sky

"It should be a happy place. I really love it, it is gorgeous and it's in a beautiful wood near the river and all I can do is cry every time I go there," she admitted as she asked me to come and clear her family cabin near Sedona, AZ.

We set a time to meet and when I approached, a woman I did not know came on the porch and said,

"Don't sit there or there," pointing to the two rocking chairs. The woman swayed with a bottle in her hand. I could smell the alcohol from a distance. She disappeared inside and I didn't see her again.

I had already sensed the two Native Americans in the rockers who now came into my inner vision. I inquired internally and was told one was the chief and the other his son. They were waiting for me. I nodded to each and waited until Matty came to the door.

Red around her tired eyes told me she had done her fair share of crying today. I could hear the creek's song from the porch. The cabin was two stories plus a basement. I guessed it was around 3,000 square feet. Inside the rooms were all well-appointed in modern rustic comfort. The kitchen sported top-of-the-line appliances including a fan which drew smoke down and out leaving the view above clear. The wrap-around porch and beautiful gardens completed the picture.

"We have to meditate and each get the story first, independently. Then you will tell me what you get," she directed in her firm, hesitant and skeptical way. Her face was hopeful. She was more sensitive than she wished to admit even to herself. We sat on benches near the rockers occupied by two Native American spirits.

"That's fine," I agreed. She had participated in one of my Earth Healing Classes and had been one to question everything, which I found healthy.

We both sat in silent meditation. After some time, I heard the chief say,

"Metal spiders from the sky, fire out of their bellies," and I saw an image of many Native Americans running in shock, panic and chaos while spaceships with long metal legs pursued them killing them with laser rays out of the bottom of the ships. It was like a terrible page out of a Marvel comic book.

I had done some research and this was another of those people-disappeared-without-a-trace Arizona places. Previously a tribe of 1,000 Natives lived in this river valley. They had mysteriously disappeared leaving artifacts behind. This message, although surprising, fit and could be a possible answer to the mystery of their disappearance.

When the information felt complete, I opened my eyes and shortly thereafter she opened hers. She looked at me in a challenging way and asked what I got.

"Metal spiders from the sky, fire out of their bellies," I began quoting the Chief. Her face remained still but her eyes widened in recognition. I described the rest of the scene and she nodded pensively.

She had gotten slightly different words but basically the same message and the same images. We had both seen hundreds and hundreds of people mowed down in the prime of their lives. I could see the chief nodding his head as he rocked on the porch.

50

"Now what?" she asked anxious to get this resolved.

I guided all of us through a ceremony including the process of helping these souls cross over. It took a couple of hours for all of them to go, especially some that tried to evade us. The chief was last and made sure all went through before he said his thanks and disappeared into the light.

Spent and a little mind blown, I walked down to the river to put my feet in. Before I arrived, I felt blocked by the energy of some very tall spirits. I asked who was there and was shown Metatron and two Hathors. I communed with them for a time, appreciated their gratitude for what we had done. Cooling my feet in the chilly water I contemplated, as Douglas Adams would have said, "Life, the Universe and Everything."

The woman later reported that she had no more tears at the cabin. She was finally able to sleep and enjoy the beauty around her when there.

EARTH HEALING SEMINAR 2022

check
www.BodySoulandAngels.com
for details on the next class

GOALS: to come together to comtem-
plate Earth Healing and your place in it;
to share/discuss ideas, issues, projects;
to develop intuitive abilities/enhance
your skills to help Gaia; to support each
other as a community; to learn through
stories, information and discussions.

Lyneahmarks@gmail.com

Chapter 11

Luthier Man

Charlie Mason was a West Virginia country gentleman, a mighty fine finish carpenter and in later years became a luthier (a string instrument builder). He mostly built lap and hammered dulcimers and occasionally antique replicas just to prove he could. He was the grandfather I never had. It was a privilege working with him for three years full time. Despite his limited formal education, he was one of the wisest people I've known.

Originally, I went to him to ask if he would teach me to build a lap dulcimer. It had become important to me to know things from beginning to end, so I wanted an instrument that I built myself. When I first stopped by his place, we talked for quite some time and got along well. His wife was another story. Cold and distant, she didn't want "foreigners" in her living room. Being from out of state we qualified. I gave him my contact information not hoping for anything. A few months later I answered the phone and heard,

"My wife's gon' an' killed herself," in a rather matter of fact way. He went on to explain that she was an epileptic and fell on the cement steps and "crushed her skull" and was not expected to live much longer.

"Give me a little time to settle my affairs after she passes and then it will be time to come build a dulcimer because I will need company," he concluded.

I offered condolences, watched the newspaper for her obit, attended the funeral and he thanked me for coming saying he'd call soon. He did. We developed a wonderful friendship and I started cooking for him and cleaning in addition to learning to build a dulcimer. I worked with him for three years, built 50 musical instruments, repaired others, attended county fairs and arts & crafts shows. He died very suddenly and left a big hole in my life.

It took some time before I was able to play dulcimer in a concert. We had been asked to perform at the high school for a festival and I thought I was ready to be able to play without crying. One of the songs I played was Redwing. After I finished, I felt a tap on my shoulder like someone was tapping me with a hammered dulcimer hammer. Charles often did that in life. I turned and there he was standing next to me.

"Girl, it goes like this…" he played over the strings and accented one note I had missed. "Now you do it." I repeated the phrase correctly and he said,

"That's the way. Now do it that way again." I held back tears, turned to the band and said,

"Let's do Redwing again." We did and I did it right.

A couple of years later, someone came over saying he had inherited a dulcimer that needed to be repaired. He had tracked me down through folks in town. He pulled his truck up the hill and carried in a lovely cherry wood table style hammered dulcimer that was clearly Charlie's creation. He brought it into the house and while I worked on it, he went back outside. He had inherited the instrument from a relative and had never met Charlie. Before long he came in and asked if I knew anyone who wore a green Sears and Roebuck's work suit.

"He was dressed all in green work clothes and walked with his hands behind his back. He looked maybe 65 years old and he said, 'That girl will take good care of you. Tell her I said Hi.'"

"That's Charlie!"

Many people have visits from recently departed relatives and friends. Whenever I tell a story like this one, many people come up afterward to tell me their version. It's way more common than most people think because many people feel it is weird and are unwilling to share unless they meet someone who is comfortable with the subject.

Rudolf Steiner's Meditation Techniques Teaches Us Mindful Meditation

Exercise 3: Equanimity - Here we try to avoid swinging between sympathy and antipathy toward what comes to us from outside. Instead we try to maintain a balance between the two extremes. By consciously paying attention to our reactions we come to see how letting ourselves be swayed from side to side prevents us from seeing the true nature of what meets us. We become more receptive to what lives in our environment if we avoid extreme expressions...continued at

http://www.bodysoulandangels.com/five-basic-exercises

Chapter 12

This House For Sale

Stark sunlight shone harshly through the naked windows of the skeleton of my childhood home. Dents, scratches, and sun-bleached spaces outlining where the furniture had been flooded memories into my consciousness.

"I stood right there for my senior prom pictures. I stepped on my older brother's watch right there as revenge for unjust public embarrassment," I thought as I looked around. I imagined my reflection in the white rectangle where the mirror had hung, and a younger version of me looked back. The empty piano space held hours of practice, the empty TV wall was bare and memories of the way the chairs used to crowd to the sides making space for the annual Christmas tree on its pedestal appeared in my mind. My original bedroom, later my parents', stood empty to the side. I turned toward the hall, passed the bathroom and came into the empty dining room.

"The dining room table was here where I sat with Gram the summer before she died," I remembered. The old tan wall phone across the dining room reminded me of the conversation which brought me here at this time.

"This house just won't sell," Mom confided in a sullen voice. "It's been on the market a year now, and it's not the neighborhood. We've had three ready, willing and able buyers until something happened to each one. The Johnsons put their earnest money down and just three days before the closing, a dreadful automobile accident hospitalized them both," I waited in silence until Mom continued.

"The Jacksons wanted the house until their son was diagnosed with leukemia. The Millers were next, and they were so interested. They talked about renting the upstairs to make half their mortgage and how good that would be. Three days before closing Mr. Miller fell from a building at work and Workers' Comp is fighting the case. He'll be in recovery a long time fighting for his benefits."

It took three incidents to make Mom believe something was going on with the house. She let the silence explain the fear she was unable, or unwilling, to verbalize. Mom felt a sense of guilt over the mishaps. She would not put the house on the market again until this was cleared up because she would not be responsible for another family's tragedy. I understood the silence and chose not to address it aloud.

"What would you have me do, Mother?" I asked quietly.

"Please come and well, check it out. You always know what to do. Just come and see what you feel."

"I don't have a clue what to do."

"Please, just come," Mother spoke with the confidence that I would figure it out.

"OK," I said, finding it impossible to say no to my Mother. "I'll have to clear some time from work, and it's busy now. I'll see what I can do. I'll call you when I know something definite," I hung the receiver heavily on its cradle. I was past the time of avoiding extra-sensory experiences, but not yet ready to openly embrace the metaphysical world publicly.

Don and I drove to Chicago. I came to say goodbye to my childhood home and out of a desire to console Mom. This was the first time I'd been in the house when it was empty.

"Lots of memories here, aren't there?" Mom's question snapped me back to the present.

"Yes, Mom, many."

A squeaky board in the dining room reminded me of my teen years late-night entries, when I tiptoed noiselessly past my parent's room, pausing long enough for Mom's breathing to shift in her sleep indicating she knew I was home. Then I tiptoed through the dining room avoiding the squeaky board, past Grandma's accordion door bedroom to the right, then to the left around the dining room table arriving at the basement door where I thought I was safe until I'd hear my grand-mother's "tch, tch, tch, tch, tch,": her tongue-clicking disapproval for all things unacceptable. I imagined her sitting in her spot at the dining room table, completing her daily crossword puzzles, two a day (Chicago Tribune and the Sun–Times) until she turned 90 when she slowed to just one a day.

Echoed footsteps in the tomb-like emptiness of my Grandmother's room ran a chill up my spine. I tried to center, relax and be comfortable enough to allow myself to open to experience something. Images of the green easy chair where the Germanic queen spent many hours, telling her Cubbies how to play baseball, the tilt of the mirror just so, no dust anywhere, all drawers in order. The idea of my Grandmother impeding the sale of this house from beyond was logically impossible but intuitively sane. How did my Mother expect me to liberate 75 years of family history?

I heard no one close by, so I sat cross-legged on the floor, closed my eyes, pushed the whirlpool of memories aside and took deep breaths. I tried to center using my meditation training. I cleared my mind and focused. I began to relax.

"No luck yet?" barked Dad in his best Archie Bunker style, shaking me from my reverie. "I knew this was a bunch of bunk bringing you here all the way from West Virginia," his words seemed to hack through the air with his bent forward posture which begged an argument. His crossed arms a reflection of his closed mind.

59

I took the time to return to calm. Dad shifted from one foot to the other, uneasy with the time my response was taking. His posture became less aggressive and a little worried.

"I haven't really begun yet. I was lost in memories of how it used to be. It's going on three years since Grandma died."

Shifting his posture again he stepped back and changed his attitude. He lowered his arms to his sides, nodded and exited without a word. Letting go of this house was not easy for any of us.

Relief turned to apprehension as I returned to the task at hand. Why was this house not selling? To relieve the stale air, I pushed and pulled until the swollen paint gave way, the window jerked upward, and fresh air washed into the room. I looked around once more and in my heart I said goodbye. I sat on the floor, centered again and let the question fill my heart and overflow throughout my being:

"Grandma? Why will this house not sell?" I waited in silence for several long minutes. Ready to leave and report that I had tried but failed, I stood up, and a sensation on my back urged me forward. At first, I thought it was imagination. I moved to the right, and the sensation urged me left. I moved to the left, and it nudged me to the right. I stepped backward and the sensation increased, pushing me firmly forward. I allowed the invisible hand to guide me out of Grandma's room, through the dining room, down the dark tunnel of a staircase into the cavernous basement where I paused. The push continued to lead me across the laundry room and halfway down the long hallway. At the huge old furnace, it directed me to the left, though the workshop, into a storage room filled with identical silver-handled white cabinets: six deep, three high on each side. Thirty-six alabaster statues whispered of treasure hunts past. Surely, the treasures had been removed. I was guided to one cabinet and the sensation stopped. I drew a deep breath and opened it. A pyramid of fragile, antique parchment scrolls filled the shelf. Curious at first, I recognized them as

beautiful hand painted birth, baptismal and marriage certificates I had studied in years past to learn about my family's history. Gold seals and lovely calligraphy, surrounded by hand painted seraphim and cherubim, dating to the 1880's. I cradled the bundle of parchments reverently in my arms as I climbed back up the stairs.

"Mom, were you going to leave these here?" I asked with incredulity gently lying them on the kitchen counter.

"Junk!" replied my Mother. "I've had old stuff around me all my life. Do you realize I lived in my Mother's home from birth 'till age 67? I like my new apartment with new furniture and new things. No old junk!"

I stared at my Mother with disbelief. We had very different points of view. Don and I loaded the precious antique items and headed home.

Grandmother

*****

"Hello? Oh hi, Mom what's up?" I asked from the comfort of my West Virginia home. Mom was excited.

"You won't believe it! The house is sold! They were preapproved and ready to go. We've already closed!"

This was my first conscious Energy Clearing and Elevation (ECE™™) or what is popularly known nowadays as a house clearing.

If there were cause and effect here and not just coincidence, how does a 93–year–old woman manipulate physical reality three years after she's dead? And, by the way, according to Goggle Earth street view, the house burned down and no one's ever rebuilt on that lot on the West side of Chicago.*

(*This chapter appears in full in *Thirsting for a Raindrop*, Lyneah Marks, Body, Soul & Angels Publishing, Chapter 30, available on Amazon.)

Chapter 13
In Search of Enlightenment

From Thirsting for Joy, Chapter 24:

"Here, this is for you," spoke one of my clients, standing with her husband next to a display cabinet poking out of the back of their truck bed. "My husband found it by the side of the road and was told to pick it up and bring it to you."

"That's interesting; I don't know where I'm going to put it and I don't know why I need it but I asked and got, '*Yes, take it.*'"

That happened in Durham, before I even had a thought of moving to Arizona. When we loaded the truck in North Carolina, strong guidance indicated I was to bring the display case with me. I stored it in the garage, still not knowing what to do with it. It was glass on the top and sides, with two glass half shelves and a full floor with wooden storage space underneath. I had no plans to open a store here despite the urgings of one of Marc's friends.

The Arizona Enlightenment Center had become a source of inspiration: a place to meet people, a place to offer energy healing work, Soul Integration including past life healings, teaching classes and leading ceremonies. The center had moved into a renovated gas station building. It had many rooms which we converted into treatment rooms, a large room for group meetings and space for a store near the front. Many people helped. It was a community of healers and those interested in healing painted and readied the place. Two members started the store. I walked in to see if I could help and said,

"Oh, I know exactly what goes in that space." The cabinet from North Carolina fit perfectly and was just what they were looking for. They placed the expensive items in this case since it locked. The Enlightenment Center had a code lock on the entry door and many people had that code. Inside, the gift shop had a separate lock and only the three shopkeepers had keys. Open wooden shelves to the right of the door had rows of homeopathic bottles ten across and five deep. Other shelves had books, musical instruments, crystals and locally made hand-made items.

Opening the shop one morning, Terry found a neat row of bottles on the floor in front of the wooden shelves. One of each of ten bottles stood on the floor in a neat row. Checking the shelf, she found each row had four bottles exactly where they belonged. The bottles on the floor had to be the last bottles from each row behind the undisturbed bottles.

"Curious," she thought. While returning the bottles to the shelf, she pondered why anyone would do that. She didn't have a hypothesis and kept the incident to herself.

The next day another of the shopkeepers, Joy, opened the store and found a small round glass tabletop overturned with all the hand-painted scarves and small pocketbooks upside down in the middle of the floor. She called Terry, who had locked up the night before and received assurance everything was in order at the time she left. She explained about finding the bottles on the floor the morning before.

Terry made sure all things were in order when she left that night; she came in to open the next morning to find all the items from the second shelf inside the locked cabinet overturned onto the shelf below. Nothing was broken. This time a little freaked out, she called the director, who told her to call me.

"What do you want me to do?" I asked.

"Heather said you would know what to do," said Terry, a little nervously.

"OK," I said hesitantly. "I'll see what I can do."

n meditation I asked who was there and did not have to wait long. A hirty-something good-looking dark-haired man presented himself in ny inner sight.

"*What do you want?*" I asked calmly.

"*I want Enlightenment, of course, you are the Enlightenment Center, aren't you?*" he asked with an edge of annoyance. "*I've been trying to get your attention for a while now.*"

This brought a smile.

"*How can we provide enlightenment for you?*"

He communicated through images now – an automobile accident on the nearby highway indicating he died in the crash. The rest came in "knowings". His distress over how his family was doing without him was his major concern. He didn't know how to find them.

I tuned in, asked my guides to help me and found the Akashic Records of his family since his death. I showed him and when he saw his family had gone through their mourning and were now doing fine, he relaxed and realized it was OK. I felt a rush of emotions followed by relief. Calm followed.

"*Are you willing to cross over now?*" I asked.

He nodded his consent. I asked angels to help him and spiritual beings opened a portal of golden yellow light and helped him across. In the light I saw people greeting him. It felt beautiful and peaceful. The Enlightenment Center had no further poltergeist activity. There was a great sense of joy at being able to help a spirit in distress find peace. What an amazing thing to be able to do for someone. I was then guided to clear the area of the accident along the highway and saw in inner sight a dark cloud transform, turning bright and dissolving. I sat in a prayer of gratitude feeling great joy.

Be careful what you name your center!*

* Thirsting for Joy, Chapter 24, Lyneah Marks, Body, Soul & Angels Publishing, 2021 available on Amazon.

Chapter 14

Good Ol' Boys

In the late 1980's, while teaching German at a Waldorf school, I made the lovely trek to Maggie Valley, near Ashville, NC for a faculty retreat. We all stayed in a large old white side boarded farmhouse complete with a wraparound porch. The first night I got no REM sleep at all. I was very tired when I went to bed and slept almost immediately after laying my head on the pillow. However, all night long, I kept having very vivid dreams that someone was trying to wake me up. I had brought my lap dulcimer with me and there were a bunch of good old boys' spirits who wanted me to get up and play the dulcimer so they could dance and party. Sleepily I kept telling them to go away as if in a dream. At one point I felt one grab my foot and shake it and I realized I wasn't dreaming. I went to the bathroom, came back and tried to sleep once more. It was almost daylight. At best I had some restless relaxation but I never fully went into a deep sleep. In the morning I felt exhausted. As I walked out of my room another teacher coming out of her room opposite me, looked equally exhausted and with a wry smile said,

"Oh, it looks like they were bothering you too!" purveying me through her swollen and sleepy eyes.

"What? The good ol' boys? Were they trying to get you to party too?" We had a tired laugh and headed for the shared dorm style bathroom. These ghosts were not interested in crossing over. They were happy, seemed drunk and wanted to party. At the time I didn't really know what to do with them except to request that my angels keep them out of the house so that we* could sleep that night. That request was honored and we both got some sleep. No one else in the group was able to sense them and nobody had any ideas of what to do with them. This was during a period when I was not working with ghosts consciously.

I don't think I've ever been back physically or energetically to clear them from that house. Maybe that could be a class project for the Ghost Guiders Webinar.

If you have something that goes bump in the night and want a consultation for ECE™ or for personal growth, **the first 20 minutes are free for first time clients.** Contact me at

Lyneah@bodysoulandangels.com.
Facebook like: Body, Soul & Angels

Chapter 15

House Clearings

After my divorce, a friend offered to do a house clearing for me. She brought her drum and went through the house clearing and blessing each room. I was very impressed with how different the house felt after this process. When she moved out of the area, I decided to learn how to offer this as a service. I was guided to purchase a rattle that contains high vibration crystals and have used it ever since as one of my main clearing tools. I use it instead of sage at ceremonies as well. I prefer it to smoke. Small Tibetan metal bowls, crystal bowls, crystals, chimes and eventually my beautiful drum made up my house clearing kit. I called it ECE™™, Energy Clearing and Elevation™. Later, I learned how to do house clearings remotely using Google Earth.

Since that time, I have completed many house clearings including ones that have resulted in houses on the market for over a year selling within days of the clearing. There are many house clearings I have done and many have had objective verification of successful changes. For example, one house that I cleared I found two rooms where the energy felt thick and stuck. Both rooms upset my stomach. When I explained what I sensed, the owner of the house told me her dog only threw up in those two rooms. I cleared very heavy energy from those rooms. She later learned a person who was dying had been cared for at home in those two rooms. The dog didn't throw up at all after this clearing. In one bedroom I felt a dark wet energy that went way down into the earth. It felt like a big wet hole. I recommended some things that they could do to protect themselves from that energy. Later they found out that there was an old well the room had been built over.

*****

Once I was hired by a woman friend who had started a new relationship with a recently divorced man. He didn't believe in this sort of thing and he followed me around with a very skeptical look on his face. His mother was even worse. I welcomed him to join me. When I got to the children's playroom I felt angry energy. I started to hear the arguments. It was after the children were in bed when they were cleaning up the playroom.

"This is where you and your wife fought," I informed him.

He never answered but he turned a little pale and had quite a look of surprise on his face. The arguments hung in the walls as a heavy dark energy and I could actually hear what they were saying. I started to quote words to him and his face indicated he didn't want to hear anymore. He swiftly disappeared and quit following me around. I completed the clearing and the blessing of each room. My friend reported later that he had been shaken by my words because they were accurate.

Many times, there are more things to clear than ghosts. There were many entities in this house that were created by the arguments, the anger and the other negative emotions. Once those were cleared, the room was comfortable and felt less like ghosts occupied it. My friend did not stay in a relationship with him long but we were both glad for the children that Energy Clearing and Elevation (ECE™™) helped provide a healthier space for them.

*****

The friend who hired me to clear her boyfriend's house had been through a miserable divorce herself. Her husband was mentally and emotionally unstable and until he was medicated, her life was quite a nightmare. At the time she was more of a colleague and also a bit skeptical about the process of ECE™™. True skeptics, as William Bengtsson observes, are more open-minded than people who have opinions or are believers or nonbelievers. After I completed ECE™™ on her house, her ex-husband, who had stayed in his vehicle when

70

bringing the children to the door after sporting events, asked if he could come in and have a cup of tea for the first time since their separation. He did something that she never expected him to ever do: he apologized. He apologized to her for his previous behavior.

Clearing out the old can make way for something new to come in and in this case it did. Their relationship improved from angry cold exchanges to a much more civil level and this too provided a healthier environment for the children. Many other clearings have had similar results.

Rudolf Steiner's Meditation Techniques Teaches Us Mindful Meditation

Exercise 4: Positivity - To cultivate this soul attitude does not mean to avoid all criticism or to close our eyes to what is bad, false, or inferior. It is not possible to find the bad good and the false true. It does mean to attain an attitude of sympathetically entering into any situation so as to see its best attributes. It means responding to what is praiseworthy, seeking out what is to the good, constructive, beautiful in all things and situations.

Chapter 16

Dental Ghost

A long-term client asked me to clear her husband's dental office. We went in after hours because the husband didn't believe in ECE™™ and not to disturb the practice. I didn't know anything about the history of this office when we started. I offered her a choice of a dual chime or a small Tibetan bowl to use for clearing and I used my rattle. She took the challenge of playing the Tibetan bowl. The office had many rooms and the main hallway went around in a circle. She learned that the bowl was an indicator of the state of the energy in the room. The denser the energy, the less the bowl would sustain a note.

We started in the reception room, I went first and she followed. As the rattle cleared the space her bowl played better and better. We cleared the reception room fairly quickly and the bowl sounded loud and long. We went on to each of the treatment rooms which took more time to clear. When I came to the back of the hall it was as if an invisible wall was there. I felt resistance to going through the area outside the file room.

"What's going on here?" I asked

"That's what we want to know. Everyone avoids going through this area. It's funny to watch. Staff and patients walk all the way around instead of going through this area."

After tuning in for a time, I saw a body lying on the floor in my inner sight. It appeared to be dead. It was a large male, older than high school age but not yet a full adult. As I tuned into the scene, I saw another man, a little older, standing over him and I felt great waves of fear. I got the idea that the two people had broken into the office to use laughing gas and one had overdosed. His friend pulled him by the feet and dragged him out into the yard behind the building. I asked,

"Do you know if anyone died in here?"

"Well, I don't know about in here, but there was a man. The police said he was found out back. It was before we owned this building. My husband purchased it from a retiring dentist. There was a man who was found dead in the backyard. He was a young man probably in his late teens or early 20s. They think he overdosed on nitrous oxide."

"Try playing the bowl over here," I pointed to the area in question. She was not able to make it sing. Neither could I. "When a bowl like this doesn't ring, it means the energy is dense."

I suggested she get the chimes and we went to work to clear the space. The rattle and chimes cleared the space after some work.

"Try the bowl again," I suggested. This time the bowl rang clear and loud, sustaining the sound.

"Success," I concluded. I shared what I had seen in my vision and she said that made sense. It could have happened that way because the back door was broken into according to the police report.

Next, we created sacred space and sat close to the clearing area. We tuned in asking if the spirit had crossed over. Getting a no feeling, we started working together to help him cross over. Suicides have a special ICU in the spiritual world to help them prepare to transition. We called in suicide angels for assistance and worked with him until he went with them.

Later my friend reported that people now walked through the area with ease. They were totally unaware their behaviors had changed. The office workflow improved and my friend felt so much better about the space. Many were affected but few were conscious of what was happening.

I guess it's like any of the senses. Some people can perceive minute differences in colors and others are color blind. Some people can hear frequencies above a dog whistle and others can't. A sommelier has fine abilities to detect differences in wine tastes and others think any wine is ok. Also, we tend to ignore that which we don't understand. The Hitchhiker's Guide to the Galaxy calls it "somebody else's problem". Many perceive ghosts but are not interested in exploring their subtle perceptions because they do not understand or because fear gets in the way: fear of being ridiculed by others, fear of not knowing what to do, fear of the unknown, fear stimulated by scary movies. Fear is the opposite of love and when fear is cleared, love can flow.

Chapter 17

Little Boy in Shower

Children are often more sensitive to the presence of ghosts than adults who have had more time to deny their perceptions. The majority of our educational systems focus on the development of our brain's logical side and do nothing to nurture our intuitive side. In fact, they do much to discourage our intuitive abilities. Both sides are important to our survival.

I have often said that the first part of my formal education trained my logical brain and I have spent the rest of my life training my intuitive side. Clients who have learned that I am intuitive and have a metaphysical outlook often call me for help with the unusual. One client, a Mom, called and said,

"Since we moved into this house, Brandon has become afraid of sleeping in his room." There was a long pause and a long sigh before she said, "I have recently learned he is seeing a man in his bedroom and he often comes into the bathroom when Brandon is showering. He is a young 7 and a very sensitive child but he's never been afraid to sleep in his room before. Can you come and help us please?"

We set a time and when I arrived, Brandon was not there. I meditated for an hour and the ghost didn't appear. I ran out of time and had to come back again and this time both children were playing in an adjoining room. I got Brandon's permission to sit in his room, meditated and asked the ghost to show himself. I felt him much closer this time. After some chit chat about his drawings, I asked,

"Brandon, your Mom tells me you have a visitor in your room sometimes," he nodded his head. "Can you describe him for me?" He was shy about it.

"I used to have a little boy in my home. He was sad." He looked at me for a time and then said,

"He is a tall man in a black suit. He doesn't wear a tie, but he could. He seems dressed up. He's sad. He tries to talk with me and I don't want to hear him."

"Has he ever told you his name? He shook his head in the negative.

"What do you want to happen?"

"I want him to go away and stop bothering me. I'm just a kid. I don't know how to help him. He seems to want help. I'm the only one who can see him."

"That's because you have special abilities some people don't have. Most of my family couldn't see spirits either, just me and once in a while one of my cousins."
He looked relieved.

"I'll try to talk with him and find out how we can help him so he doesn't bother you anymore."

"Good." He said quickly as he returned to the other room to color.

I sat for a quiet meditation and eventually a man came forward in my inner perception.

"Hello," I said to him quietly inside my head. He startled, surprised I could see him. "I'd like to talk with you."

"What do you want?" he inquired almost philosophically calming himself after the initial startle response.

"I'm here to find out what you want."

"I'm not sure. I used to live here with my wife. "

"What are you feeling?"

"Oh, that's easy, I am sad."

"What are you sad about?"

He launched into a story about how his wife was cold and used sex as a weapon. She was almost never available for sex and was not affectionate. He was a musician and a sensitive man. He didn't mean to, but he became involved with a younger musician and they had a sweet affair.

"It sounds like you are also feeling guilt."

"Oh, yes, a lot of guilt," he said looking down at his hands now wringing each other.

"Can you feel compassion for yourself?"

"I haven't considered that."

I led him through some inner child work and helped him apply compassion for himself. I helped him find understanding instead of judgment. After a time, I asked if he had considered going into the light.

"Oh, no, I don't want to see my wife. That's why I didn't go and now the portal isn't open. I am afraid of her and I'm afraid of judgement."

"Well, as far as I've seen, we are our own worst judges. It's more about what you have learned and how you can digest this life's lessons."

We talked at length. He was an intelligent, sensitive man. Eventually, I asked angels if they could arrange for him not to see his wife and they agreed to protect him. It took some time to convince him and counter his various objections but eventually he agreed to cross over. The angels opened a portal and he went into the light, no sign of his wife. The portal closed and the little boy didn't see him again.

Each time I help someone it is different in the details, but the process is similar. Connect with the Disembodied Spirit and ask what their story is. Listen openly. Apply the techniques you have been trained to use and help them resolve their roadblock so they can cross over. Ask for spiritual help. If the spirit doesn't want to go, well, we'll look at that in the next chapter.

Chapter 18

A Reluctant one

We moved into an older neighborhood in North Carolina in 2006, a community built for relocated IBM workers back in the early 60's. We found two homes of identical design: one built in the '60s, the other, built a decade later, used less-sturdy materials. We chose the 60's house.

After we moved in, we discovered that the couple next door were avid Duke fans. They had moved into their house in the 60's and never left.

"When we moved here we came in a red 1964 Corvette Sting Ray. It was a beaut!" he informed us. This couple was well into their retirement years but I could imagine her in a cheerleader's pleated skirt and him in a letterman's sweater. They told us of the couple who had lived in our house from the 60's until 2 years before we arrived. Like many, they had stayed in this community until they died or had to be taken to a care facility.

We cleared the house we moved into. Some renters had brought disruptive energies and opened an interdimensional portal which had to be closed.

I liked to drive past the lake going in and out of the community. A great blue heron lived in the pond on one side of the road. One day he was there as I drove by and I paused to get a better look at him. While doing so I noticed a new family moving into a house on the lake a few doors down. Their van advertised a church. The father looked like a preacher and they had several children.

Several days later, I stopped again to watch the Great Blue Heron catch a fish. I heard racial slurs. I looked around and there was no one there. The next day I heard them again as I drove past the house with the new family. I ignored them for several days not fully certain where the phrases were coming from. Finally, I stopped and asked who was there. An older looking man appeared. I didn't have to ask what he wanted. He wanted this Black family out of what had been his house.

"This is no longer your house. You are dead. It is 2006," I said to him silently. He was not fazed.

"I don't care, I want them out!" He continued in no uncertain terms to demand this family leave.

I tried every way I could to convince him he no longer had the right to impose his energies on this family to no avail. I spoke with him about karma and he wasn't impressed. I quoted him scripture and that had no effect. I offered the Golden Rule and he stayed stuck on his attitude, energy and demands.

Finally, I asked my guides what I could do to help and was told that since he was violating the free will of this family, I could contain him so they would not be affected by his energies. To do this without creating karma for myself, I needed to have equanimity of soul, meaning that I had to not enjoy this, not feel revengeful or any unbalanced emotion such as anger. I needed to feel that this was for his best interest since he was accumulating negative karma for himself. I asked for assistance and was given help to contain him in a plexiglass container and lovingly ask angels to watch over him until he was willing to cross over. Every time I have told this story I have checked in n him. In 2022 I finally saw that he had crossed over.

Rudolf Steiner's Meditation Techniques Teaches Us Mindful Meditation

Exercise 5: Open Mindedness - By whatever regulating forces we have been living heretofore, and are used to -beliefs, customs, laws --we should keep ourselves ready at any moment to take in a new idea, a new experience, with total impartiality. Life is continually evolving, sometimes at a rapid pace, and we need to see what is for the good and what is detrimental to it; also how we are to proceed in relating to it. New manifestations of truth must find us ready at any time to receive them...for more information, see: http://www.bodysoulandangels.com/five-basic-exercises

Chapter 19

GUYS DANCING UPSTAIRS

"This pain began after we moved into this house. It has persisted and my chiropractor, normally very effective, hasn't been able to help me. We've been in the house two months and it all seems to be getting worse. My daughter has had attitude issues and severe mood swings since we moved in. I know it has something to do with the house. When can you come and clear it? We need help," concluded the lady I met.

"I can come later today." We made arrangements.

As I approached, the home was a Desert Tuscan Style, one story with ample square footage. It could only have been a few years old. It looked attractive from the outside which was well kept. When I stepped in, I expected a bright living room but despite the more than ample windows and the sunny desert day, the room felt like being in a dark, damp cave. A Labrador retriever skulked on the other side of the room eying me suspiciously. I had never seen a lab act this way before.

"I'm sorry, but I have to sit because of the pain in my back," the lady of the house apologized. Her daughter walked quickly through the room giving me an angry sort of look and disappeared into the back of the house.

"I'm sorry again. My daughter has been very angry and rude since we moved here."

85

I nodded and decided to focus on the dog first. This was very unusual behavior for a lab. I did my opening and went into inner sight, I saw something I had never seen before on the dog's back. The closest thing It reminded me of were the monkeys in the Wizard of Oz but without clothes.

I commanded it to get off the dogs back. It immediately sprang out; the dog came to me and licked my feet with a total change in attitude. The dog sat at my feet and thumped its tail leaning against me. Petting the dog to reassure her, I made sure my protection was strong and made it clear none of them were to get on me. I started seeing beings like the first one all over the room including one on the back of the woman and one on her daughter. I asked internally what was going on and what I could do to correct it.

I was guided to a fractured portal in the fireplace that was a crack between dimensions. These beings were here as a result of this rupture and I was to repair the portal, install check valves and use a form of energetic bait to draw all of these beings back to their home dimension. I asked them if they didn't miss home and many reply 'yes' and showed an emotional shift. They voluntarily went through the portal. I next worked on the ones on the mother and daughter's backs, then the beings throughout the house. Many went through the portal. There were hundreds in the neighborhood and the city and when I extended it to the world, thousands left.

When I was complete I explained what I had seen and what I had done.

"That's really interesting. There was only one owner here before us. She was an older woman who lived alone and after two years she put the house on the market. Everyone in the neighborhood thought she was crazy because she used to complain that she couldn't sleep because of the guys dancing upstairs. As you can see, there is only one story but now I think she meant on the roof. By the way, my back feels great. Thank you so much."

Her daughter came in and talked with us in a most civil manner. She said she felt better and didn't know why. Her mother said she'd explain later. The living room now felt comfortable like a beautiful sunlit Tuscan Desert room should.

Not everything that disturbs us is a ghost.

EARTH HEALING SEMINAR 2022

check
www.BodySoulandAngels.com
for details on the next class

GOALS: to come together to comtem-
plate Earth Healing and your place in it;
to share/discuss ideas, issues, projects;
to develop intuitive abilities/enhance
your skills to help Gaia; to support each
other as a community; to learn through
stories, information and discussions.

Lyneahmarks@gmail.com

Chapter 20

Group Clearings

My husband Marc and I lived in North Carolina and often traveled to Baltimore to visit relatives. We were guided to drive different ways and many times we would come across battlefields. The battlefields contained ghosts and at each place we would be given different techniques to help with the clearing. One of the largest ones was Antietam, Maryland. 23,000 killed, wounded or missing after 12 hours of battle. They say the rivers ran red with blood.

When I saw the numbers involved I knew we didn't have enough time to help all of them across so I asked intuitively for a technique that would work. What I saw in my inner sight was quite a scene. Etheric tents were placed all around the edges of the battlefield in a large U shape. Tables under the tents had chairs along each side. Pewter scrying bowls filled with water were placed between each pair of chairs. I was guided to call in angels to help. At each set of chairs one Union soldier faced a Confederate soldier on the other side. Angels at each spot showed images in the scrying bowls from their past lives. In most cases they had killed each other many lifetimes. When they saw how long this had been going on they wanted to know how to end this pattern. They were given advice and then guided to cross over. This clearing continued for a week and I tuned in to it from a distance making sure everything was proceeding smoothly. At the end of the week there was a feeling of release, relief and completion.

We have cleared many battlefields and we know teams that do
this work regularly. I also know there are many individuals and
groups who we don't know that do this work. Many people are
reluctant to talk about it.

Cemeteries are often places to do group clearings. One graduate
of my Earth Healing Classes is a truck driver who is often
guided on roads with cemeteries. This happened so frequently
that we developed a Cemetery Macro, which saves time. See
www.bodysoulandangels.com for times for the Creating
Macros Webinar.

Hospitals and nursing homes can often use clearings and help
getting souls to cross over. What other places can you think of
for these types of clearings?

Sites of massacres offer opportunities for group clearing. I had a
series of events lead me to going to a fire ceremony on the way
to Castle Lake near Mt. Shasta, CA. I was informed before I
went that there had been a massacre of a Native tribe there. The
night of the fire ceremony, Olga, the facilitating Shaman, asked
me to deal with the darkness over by the trees. I found the
massacred Native tribe spirits standing under the trees in the
shadows. I sat down and communicated with the chief who
said he was weary and open to the possibility of crossing over.

Olga facilitated a lovely fire ceremony and when she asked for
what others had, I waited till last and invited the tribe to come
close to the fire. My guidance was to read the Akashic records
which showed them as Nordic marauders in a past life. The
massacre had been karmic. This is not always the case, but in
this case the chief saw the reality of the akashic record and was
remorseful for what they had previously done. This allowed
them to let go of their emotions of anger and desires for
revenge. At the end of the fire ceremony Olga opened the portal
and I invited the tribe to cross through the fire and into the

bright yellow light opening. The chief was the last to go through. It was a most memorable evening in several feet of snow at a high elevation with very cold temperatures. It's not the kind of ceremony that I would normally go to. I'm not fond of the cold after having died of hypothermia (see Thirsting for a Raindrop, Chapter Two). The guidance to go was strong though and I am very grateful to have been able to help facilitate this release. I am also grateful for foot and hand warmers!

Helpful Tool:

For This Michaelic Age
by Rudolf Steiner

"We must eradicate from the soul all fear and terror of what comes toward humans out of the future. We must acquire serenity in all feelings and sensations about the future. We must look forward, with absolute equanimity, to everything that may come and we must think only that whatever comes is given to us by a world direction full of wisdom. It is part of what we must learn in this age: to live out of pure trust, without any security in existence, trust in the ever present help of the spiritual world. Truly, nothing else will do, if our courage is not to fail us. Let us seek the awakening from within ourselves, every morning and every evening. (see next page)

MORNING:

O, Michael,
Under Your protection I place myself,
With Your guidance I connect myself,
Wholeheartedly,
So that this day may become an image
Of your destiny–ordering Will.

EVENING

"I carry my sorrow into the setting sun,
Place all my worries into her radiating
womb
Purified in love, transformed in light,
They return as helping thoughts,
As strength for self–sacrificing deeds."

Chapter 21

If You Don't Feel Yourself···

Marc and I were in Eastern North Carolina in a rural area. We had been guided to take some back roads and stopped at a produce store that had a large table of watermelon. I didn't feel like getting out of the small truck so I said,

"Please pick up a watermelon for us for lunch."

Marc agreed. After using the facilities, he looked over the watermelons and chose a very small one. I wondered why he had chosen such a small one and felt a little annoyed. He put the melon behind his seat and started to drive. I became angrier and angrier about the watermelon. I felt it was ridiculous to be angry over such a small thing, but the aggravation grew and grew. I had become not nice but then recognizing it as abnormal behavior, I mentioned it to Marc and he said,

"If you are not feeling yourself, who are you feeling?"

"Ah, yes." I responded and turned inward to find out who was on the back of the truck. There were several spirit hitchhikers. One was a woman who had a long story about being sold to a much older man. It seems she was sold to him because her family was so poor. Another was the man who was still bothering her. We convinced her that she did not need to be under his control any longer and to his upset, we helped her cross over. After she went through the portal closed. He asked to cross over since he no longer had someone to control. The angels opened a different portal for him and he crossed over. The small truck bed still seemed full. We helped Civil War soldiers cross over, farmers who had complaints about their land and wives who didn't want to see their husbands.

When you carry the light in you, spirits detect this and as they are often looking to go into the light, they attach asking for your help.

A quick change in your mood may indicate you are picking up on someone else's emotions. It is time to clear entities and facilitate the spirits finding resolution so you can go back to feeling good yourself. If you don't feel competent to do so, call someone who can assist you. Who ya gonna call?

Chapter 22

Care Required

Many years ago, when I was new at this, a colleague called asking me to clear her pre-Civil War home. She gave me the background,

It was a farmstead and then a hotel and then a private home. During the Civil War, it was turned into a hospital. Something just doesn't feel right here and I need your help to clear the property as well as the house."

We made a date to do the clearing on the following Saturday. Early Saturday morning the phone rang,

I can't do it today. The water pipe in the barn broke and I'm having to get an emergency plumber out to repair it. Can we reschedule?"

Of course, I hope it's easy to repair. Call me when you are ready to reschedule," I felt the rush in her voice so we did not speak further at that time.

We rescheduled about a week later. The water break had been repaired and the barn seemed fine. The morning I was supposed to go to her house she again called early,

The pipe in the upstairs broke and the bathroom ceiling is falling. I had to turn the water off and I have the plumber coming soon."

OK, good luck with that. I'm so sorry to hear that."
We rescheduled a third time and another water issue happened.

"You can't come."

"I have to come." I retorted before I realized what I was saying. "Let me do a few things here and I'll call you back."

I did my opening and asked if it was right action for me to clear this place. I got a loud "YES". I asked what I needed to do and in meditation I tuned in to a nasty spirit who did not want me there. He was not interested in having the place cleared nor in having my presence anywhere near there.

"I bind you in the name of Jesus the Christ! You may not cause further problems for Tina." I called her back.
"I'm coming. I've bound the spirit that is causing all this trouble."

"Oh, I get it," she said. "That's why all these things have happened. I was right, the feeling out here is creepy and getting creepier."

"Yes, and I want to come right now to deal with him and clear him and his energy from your place."

"Right, come ahead if you are still willing to. Just know you won't be able to use the downstairs bathroom."

"I'll see you in about 40 minutes," and I headed out the door. I had already packed the car.

We first grounded with Mother Earth and then we opened sacred space and used our discernment statement:

"Only those who believe Christ came in the flesh and only those who have our highest good at heart from Divine Source's point of view are welcome to help us."

We called in Jeshua, Mother Mary, Quan Yin, Baba Ji, Sanat Kamara, Lady Nada, and others that were right action to work with us. I felt a strong circle of light protecting us.

"OK, who is here?" as I asked, I felt a burst of anger and a burst of fear through the cushion of love light. I centered and aligned with my higher self, Divine source and Mother Earth once more.

It took quite some time to get the spirit to talk with me. He was very angry that he was bound and irate that I was here. There was a woman spirit who I sensed and called forward. She was terrified of him. I explained that he could not hurt her now and she slowly came forward and told her story. She explained that she was sold to him in life and he was a sexual dominant over her. He treated her as a slave and somehow he hung around until she also left her body and he enslaved her in spirit keeping her from crossing over.

"You no longer need to listen to him." I said aloud.

He shook the container the angels had placed him in.
I ensured her she had nothing to fear and that she could cross over and get away from him if she chose. She nodded her dark stringy hair vigorously with wide eyes. I asked the angels to open a portal and escort her through and they did. I felt an enormous cloud of relief when she left. She turned to wave a thank you as she crossed.

The man was furious. I asked what I could do to help. He was not open to hearing anything I had to say, he had little respect for women in general. He was not interested in crossing over. He was interested in getting his "hands" on me but I would not let him out.

Eventually, I was shown how to build a strong plexiglass container for him and he was removed to a remote area with angels to watch over him until he decided to cross over.

It took the rest of the day to clear the house, the barn and the surrounding property. Afterwards, the water systems stopped breaking. Peace was restored. Even the horses looked happier. The woman was able to continue on her spiritual path. Usually those who cross over continue their spiritual paths going through a life review and receiving helpful impulses based on their life lessons. After this, they can continue in the spirit world or plan a new earthly life depending on their karma and choices.

Chapter 23

Groups Clearing Together

I have found myself in several groups doing clearings. One was at a cemetery in Chapel Hill NC. A group of healers formed a circle during the day. Many people walked by on this busy campus. While tuning in with the group, a spirit pushed me into the circle to get my attention. We cleared many spirits that day including the one that was able to push me.

On a trip to France, I was surprised to find I had a lifetime at Chartres. As I walked up the aisle, I felt heavier. I felt like someone had placed a heavy cloak on me. I stopped, observing this phenomenon for time and asking what this feeling was. It turned out to be the heaviness of wearing a nun's full habit including the large coif. I had never realized how heavy they could be. I was not raised Catholic this lifetime. When I got to the front of the cathedral, I knelt in front of the beautiful Rose window a couple of rows back form the altar. Despite the rainy overcast day, the colors of the windows were spectacular. The entire cathedral is designed to make you feel small and it accomplishes its task brilliantly.

I asked to know more about my life at Chartres. Images and knowings came in quickly. I was the thorn in the Bishop's side. The Bishop was very concerned with building the Cathedral, since the nuns were living in the Cathedral at the time, it probably was during a reconstruction period after a fire, between 1194 -1260. The Bishop built a portion of the church and I would go to him quoting scripture and saying:

"Father, the children need shoes. They come to school barefoot even in cold weather."

The Bishop would give me funds to have shoes made for the children and then he built another part of the Cathedral. I went to him asking for food for the children who were malnourished pointing out to him that it was our Christian duty to feed the poor. He gave me a little money to make a soup kitchen.

Being energetic and curious, one day I stumbled on the stairs to the catacombs beneath the Cathedral where I saw prisoners being tortured. Horrified I ran back to my room and cried and shook from fear. Unfortunately, one of the prison guards saw me and reported this to the Bishop who slowly started poisoning my food. I became very ill and died.

As the vision continued the Bishop's spirit came before me asking forgiveness and I gave it to him saying I had lessons to learn from this. When I gave him forgiveness, a beam of golden light came through the rose window despite the overcast sky and he rode it upward. I felt great gratitude and relief from him and within myself. The golden light had to be spiritual because the sky was completely cloud covered for hours on our way to Chartres. Many souls came up from the Catacombs and said,

"If you can forgive him, so can we." These were souls that had been killed in the Catacombs. They rode the same beam of light upward toward the open portal of golden light.

My husband and I stayed in the Cathedral holding space for exiting souls for a long time. Finally, we headed for Paris. That night I received emails from our team members working with us from the States saying there were many other souls to cross over. I asked if they could oversee that project as we had a schedule we had to keep. The team did a great job holding space for that clearing and reported it took five days. How wonderful to have a team to support you on such journeys. The practicality of having to return a rental car and make a flight kept us from staying a full five days at Chartres.

What we did there opened an opportunity for many to cross over. This seems to be happening more and more. Clients who work through a past life open the door for others to heal of the same issues. How important it is for us to do our work because it makes it easier for others. I like the analogy of a path through a field of tall sturdy grass. When one person walks it the grass comes up and hides the path. When 100 people use it regularly, it creates an easier path to follow. Each one of us who does our inner work walks such a path and when enough have gone before us, we contribute to the easier passage for others who come after us. Recently, I have especially seen this with clients clearing past lives of sexual abuse. When the person clears, other spirits are better able to clear and cross over.

We have done group clearings of the prison system which have resulted in real reform. We have done group clearings at battle sites, battle ships, cemeteries, hospitals, nursing homes, prisons and former prisons to name a few. There are many opportunities to apply the techniques covered in more detail in the Ghost Guiders Webinar.

Chapter 24

Still on the Market

"Hello, Lyneah? I have a house for you to clear. It has been on the market a full year with no nibbles. I took over the contract a little more than a month ago and I'm having the same results. People are very vague about what they don't like about the house. They just say this is not the right house for them," conveyed the Realtor.

"How old is the house?" I queried.

"That's part of the mystery. It's only three years old and it's in excellent shape. It only had one previous owner who took very good care of it. The house looks brand new. It's been unoccupied for a little more than a year and on the market the entire time. The previous owners moved due to a change in employment. It has been taken care of and it is priced well in a good neighborhood with good schools. We've even lowered the price below comps and still no nibbles."

"Well, let me go over and see what I can find out," we agreed on a time and price for ECE™™.

I went over and cleared the inside energy but there wasn't much to clear. I found one little spot by the stairs where a child had a minor fall. I later got confirmation that there was a young child in the house but nothing tragic happened. There were a few Native and a few Civil War spirits that I cleared but in general the clearing and the blessing of the house elevated the energies nicely but I didn't feel the change was significant.

I completed the Energy Clearing and Elevation but I don't feel there was that much to clear," I said to the Realtor.

"I have showings in two and three days and I'll let you know what happens."

"Please do and if nothing is different I'll come back and do some further checking."

I heard from her in a few days. She reported that nothing had changed. People were still making vague statements about how it just didn't feel right or it just didn't feel like mine.

"People look at the house from the street, seem to like it and before they get in the door, they are making excuses why this is not the house for them. Nothing specific, just a general uneasiness about this house."

I went back over and started outside this time. I heard her say they didn't even get into the house before they started making excuses. I paid close attention walking up to the house and I ran into a river of black energy in the front yard. I sat on the front porch and traced it back to its origin. In my inner sight I saw an old shanty of a house. I was surprised that I recognized the house in my vision! A client lived just a few doors away from it and when I visited her, I had noticed it emitted dark, uncomfortable energy. My client who had just had surgery and was home-bound said she was afraid of that house. She said it was full of thieves and drug addicts. Now I remembered a major murderer had been arrested from that neighborhood and I suspected from that very house. I asked inside what I could do and was told that I could contain the house and that would stop the energies from leaking out into the neighborhood.

The house was more than a mile away but it must have been on a ley line connecting the two. After I contained the house with the help of angelic beings, I started clearing out the river of dark energy with the help of Saint Germain. Then I blessed the yard, the pathway, the porch

nd the front door. I went inside to do a clearing at the front door and
un Energy Elevation throughout the house one more time. This was
ompleted on a Thursday.

hat Saturday there was a bidding war on the house. It sold for more
1an market value which was considerably above the current list price. I
/as also very happy that it would help to clear the entire neighborhood
nd possibly the entire ley line. Obviously, the realtor was very happy
/ith these results.

\ friend who was flipping houses did not believe in the whole Energy
Ilearing and Elevation process. He had put his house on the market for
everal months without any interest at all. He called me saying he didn't
elieve in this process but he was going to give it a try. He helped me
/ith ECE™™ to find out what it was about. I found a Disembodied
pirit in the basement, helped him across and cleared that energy. I also
?lt some energy leakage and suggested finishing a part of the basement.
1 the meantime, I put an energetic field there to help. My friend took
otes as I told him what he could do in each area to improve the appeal
rom an energetic point of view. He did all the things I suggested. These
1ings come to me intuitively. I am not trained in Feng Shui but people
ave told me that some of the suggestions are in alignment with those
rinciples. We cleared the rest of the house which held energies from
1e former occupants who had a contentious relationship, eventually
eparation and divorce. After ECE™™ was complete and he enacted the
ecommended changes, the house sold within three days for a good
rice.

EARTH HEALING SEMINAR 2022

check
www.BodySoulandAngels.com
for details on the next class

GOALS: to come together to comtem-
plate Earth Healing and your place in it;
to share/discuss ideas, issues, projects;
to develop intuitive abilities/enhance
your skills to help Gaia; to support each
other as a community; to learn through
stories, information and discussions.

Lyneahmarks@gmail.com

AFTERWORD

EARTH HEALING AND GHOST GUIDERS

I hope you enjoyed these stories and learned something. Earth Healing, Ghost Guiders Webinars and other classes are offered when interest arises. If you are interested in participating, please contact me for more information. When classes have been scheduled, they are listed here:

http://www.bodysoulandangels.com/calendar.

I hope you have enjoyed the stories. They are all true and there are many others yet to be documented. I have learned to ask for greater protection for myself and my clients before going to do the ECE™™ (Energy Clearing and Elevation) as you may have observed in reading these stories. We cover more on this in our classes.

If you have something that goes bump in the night and want a consultation for ECE™ or for personal growth, **the first 20 minutes are free for first time clients.** Contact me at

Lyneah@bodysoulandangels.com.
Facebook like: Body, Soul & Angels

Made in the USA
Monee, IL
30 June 2022

98799607R00069